Para Tony
con afecto y aprecio
de
Jose Ugh
3-3-2014

Mañana in Cuba

THE LEGACY OF CASTROISM AND TRANSITIONAL CHALLENGES FOR CUBA

JOSÉ AZEL

authorHOUSE®

AuthorHouse™
1663 Liberty Drive
Bloomington, IN 47403
www.authorhouse.com
Phone: 1-800-839-8640

First published by AuthorHouse 2/18/2010

ISBN: 978-1-4490-7657-3 (e)
ISBN: 978-1-4490-7655-9 (sc)
ISBN: 978-1-4490-7656-6 (hc)

Library of Congress Control Number: 2010901701

Printed in the United States of America
Bloomington, Indiana

This book is printed on acid-free paper.

Institute for Cuban and Cuban-American Studies

University of Miami

Coral Gables, Florida

About the Cover

WHEN THIS PHOTOGRAPH, BY JOSÉ Azel/Aurora (cousin of the author), first appeared in the August 1991 issue of *National Geographic,* the caption read: "Telephone repairman peers beneath a flag veiling a Havana skyline hazy as Cuba's future." Today, clarity in Cuba's future is still elusive.

*To my wife Lily, who makes life better in every way,
to my son Daniel and my daughter Michelle, who
are custodians of a Cuban memory they never lived
so that someday their children, Andres, Alejandra,
and Sage, will get to know their grandfather's
homeland as a free and prosperous country.*

Contents

Foreword

A BOOK FOR THE FUTURE

In *Mañana in Cuba,* José Azel has written a magnificent book about a possible Cuban future. Since he does not want to raise the slightest doubt about his intentions, he reveals the work's objective even in the dedication: he would like his grandchildren to one day know the country of their grandfather as a free and prosperous land. He is not a political activist in search of a personal destiny, but rather, a person endowed by a clear spirit of service who has decided to donate to his compatriots a lifetime of fruitful life experiences. He left Cuba for the United States in 1961, as a thirteen-year old. In this country, he studied, obtained a Ph.D., and became a successful businessman without ever forgetting his native country.

In effect, Azel is a rare and valuable combination of an academic who has a sophisticated intellectual vision of social problems and of a successful businessman, currently retired in a comfortable lifestyle, (in which he includes adventurous sports, as he, along with his wife, are consummate mountain climbers) engaged in intense participation in North American university life at the Institute for Cuban and Cuban-American Studies at the University of Miami. Hence, he has more than sufficient credentials for his views to be taken into account.

In synthesis, what does he say? Foremost, he defends the importance of freedom as the supreme value of the Cuba that emerges from the ashes of dictatorship. Azel knows that freedom is not a byproduct of prosperity, but the opposite; it is one of the factors that promote the creation of wealth. And what is the essence of freedom? It is the possibility, enjoyed by the most prosperous and content societies in the world, to make individual decisions without outside coercions. The more that human beings can make decisions freely, the happier they will be on a personal level and the greater the benefits they will impart to society as a whole.

Naturally, Azel does not fool himself about the vastness of the problems that will be faced when change in the system finally comes to the island. He correctly reasons that, at the margin of material deprivation and as a consequence of the dictatorship, people, in order to survive, have learned to constantly lie and manipulate. At the same time, they have developed a very hostile attitude towards the public domain and a fierce individualism that sometimes excludes the most elemental forms of solidarity and altruism. For the Cuban people, the state and the collective are adversaries to be ignored.

In fact, more than half a century of collectivist dictatorship has profoundly affected the perceptions and, as a consequence, the behavior of Cuban society. As they repeat socialist dogmas, Cubans violate them all in order to survive. It is an attitude that will be very difficult to quickly eradicate once a regime change takes place. This phenomenon, by the way, is not entirely new in our history: when the Republic was established in 1902, Cubans by and large continued living with the socio-political habits acquired during the Colonial Period (embezzlement, violating the law, nepotism, electoral manipulation, etc.). This motivated thinkers like Enrique José Varona to voice the most severe warnings regarding the path the country was following. It was in those first years that the phrase "Cuba has habitants, not citizens" was popularized and since repeated a thousand times.

What response does Azel give to this extreme difficulty? How does one create a prosperous and free republic with "habitants" that lack the psychological features that characterize the leading societies in the world? This can be accomplished, according to Azel (and I share his reasoning), by way of liberal-paternalistic governments, capable of developing public policies that nudge people towards making better decisions until, little by little, Cubans create for themselves a value scale compatible with the consolidation of a stable and vibrant democracy.

In reality, this book is very timely. It was needed. It is a reflection endowed with a humanist vision that can serve as a general guide when the time of change arrives. And it is not the first time that a book, written before a historically important moment, contributes to change the fate of a nation. Juan Bautista Alberdi, the great Argentine liberal, published in 1852, shortly before the overthrow of Rosas, *Bases y puntos de partida para la organización política de la Confederación Argentina*. With it, he notably influenced the public life of his country and led the modernization of that state in a spectacular manner for the following decades. Hopefully, this work by Azel will reach a similar level of influence. It deserves to.

Carlos Alberto Montaner

Acknowledgments

THIS BOOK IS ABOUT PERSONAL reflections on a variety of topics relevant to how events may unfold *mañana* in Cuba. It represents one man's introspective thinking process as applied to Cuba's future, but it embodies the thoughts and contributions of many. It is both a solitary thinking effort and the collaborative intellectual enterprise of countless thinkers, scholars, and friends who have instructed me and have shaped my own thoughts over a lifetime in exile. Some are cited in this work; most will remain unnamed. I am profoundly grateful for all for their contributions and ideas. In particular, I want to acknowledge the tutelage of Jaime Suchlicki and his sharp editing pencil, the incisive critiques of Carlos Alberto Montaner, Orlando Gutiérrez-Boronat, Roger Medel, Carlos M. Gutierrez, James C. Cason, Brian Latell, my cousin José Azel and Andy Gomez, as well as the collaboration of my associate Vanessa Lopez, whose research and piercing commentary often influenced my thinking.

And yet, notwithstanding all this help, a work of this nature will have many shortcomings. For those, I alone am responsible.

Introduction

I WAS TEN YEARS OLD in January 1959, when the Cuban revolution came to town. Like most Cuban children, I was captivated by the circus-like and storybook qualities of that surreal experience without apprehending its tragic antecedents and consequences. It did not take long, however, for the storybook heroes to turn into villains, and by 1960, I was already involved in underground counterrevolutionary student activities. After the failure of the Bay of Pigs invasion in April 1961, my father concluded that, for our safety, my brothers and I should leave Cuba. Thus, in June 1961, I found myself in the United States as a thirteen-year-old political exile with an indelible, if juvenile, impression of how freedoms must be defended. I was never able to see my father again, and it is this heartfelt personal awareness of the importance of freedom in our lives that shapes this work.

The reflections in this book represent fifty years of experiences living and learning as a Cuban outside Cuba. They encapsulate the intellectual cosmopolitanism of having had the opportunity and good fortune to live in freedom, an opportunity denied to eleven million Cubans. It is this fortuitous cosmopolitanism that has shaped my thinking and has allowed me to appreciate that social knowledge is best conceived as the social experiences of the many and not as exercises in isolated excogitation by the few. Where knowledge is defined as being able "… to include vast amounts of unarticulated but vitally important information and conclusions, summarized in habits, aversions, and attractions as well as in words and numbers, then it is far more broadly spread through a society that when its definition … is restricted to the more sophisticatedly articulated facts and relationships."[1] This definition and understanding of social knowledge argues against selective economic changes controlled by authoritarian elitist political structures. It is a definition that argues compellingly for the empowerment of a citizenry.

Visions, Thomas Sowell tells us, "are like maps that guide us through a tangle of bewildering complexities."[2] Like maps, visions leave out many actual features. They are simplified, subjective depictions of reality. "Social visions especially must leave many important phenomena unexplained." [3] And yet, our visions of the world are essential precisely because they are the building blocks for our social, political, and economic policies. Visions have consequences. And social visions in particular are susceptible to illicit steps of inference when we fail to distinguish between knowledge and belief. Because our social visions have consequences, they require us to assess and articulate whatever reasons can be found for affirming a position. This is an intellectual, epistemic duty that this work takes very seriously. The alternative visions presented for Cuba's future matter because one will crystallize into the sociopolitical and economic narrative of the country for decades to come.

This is a book about an anti-messianic vision of a post-Castro Cuba where Cubans turn to the systemic rationality of unarticulated social experiences as the antidote to five-plus decades of messianic leadership; a vision where the characteristic of competitive political and economic systems will be considered superior to the putative special knowledge of the one (or few) in guiding the actions of the many. In other words, this is a book about finding ways to facilitate the transition from totalitarianism and a centrally planned economy to liberal democracy and a free-market economic system.

It is based on the premise that Cuban civil society has been decimated and has developed its own characteristics and inner logic as means of survival. Cuban civil society has been drained of sociopolitical energy.

---

1   Sowell, Thomas. *A Conflict of Visions: Ideological Origins of Political Struggles.* New York: Basic Books. 2007. Kindle Location 535.

2   Sowell, Thomas. Kindle location 39

3   Ibid., Kindle location 54

The capacities of the citizenry have been blunted to become engaged in self government and to take individual and collective responsibility for their lives. This work takes these adverse conditions as given, and seeks sociopolitical and economic outcomes as a function of the incentives presented to individuals, not their current dispositions. It considers how civil society interacts with incentives and seeks to offer governing policies and structures suited to the prevailing civic culture. The roadmap of Part One is as follows:

Chapter I considers the historical and cultural antecedents of Cuba's paucity of responsible citizenship behavioral patterns and how the last five decades of totalitarian rule have further distanced the Cuban population from a robust appreciation for the role of democratic institutions and civil society. It examines the Cuban intellectual disconnect between personal freedoms to choose what to do with one's life and the more abstract constructs of civil liberties and political rights. It explores the uncharacteristic stasis of conformism Cubans have adopted to escape the existential absurdity of a future without possibilities.

Chapter II notes how freedom from fear must be the first step for a genuine and successful transition, because it is a necessary condition for reversing political apathy. Freedom from fear stands out as both a means and an end. Cubans have forgotten how to feel free, and any reform effort that leaves civil society inarticulate and incapable of holding rulers accountable fails to recognize that no modern society can function in the best interest of the people without an effective system of checks and balances.

Chapter III highlights that, as we have learned in nation-building efforts throughout the world, it is easier to build new parliament buildings and courthouses than it is to populate those buildings with legislators and judges committed to democratic values and governance. Cuba's way out of its existential distress is not just freedom from deplorable economic conditions. Cuba's potentialities will depend more on individual freedoms and empowerment than on a given set of economic reforms.

Chapter IV describes how a successful Cuban transition must appreciate that the Cuban Diaspora has in fact created two distinct Cuban communities: one on the island and one in exile. It argues that this diversity embodies the best opportunity to build, in the Cuba of tomorrow, a modern politico-economic system unimpeded by the obsolete institutional structures of a communist state. The healing of the Cuban nation cannot take place in a political vacuum, it cannot take place in a totalitarian setting, and it cannot take place without the civil liberties and political rights to practice heroic tolerance and political wisdom.

Chapter V continues the discussion, noting that Cubans on the island who have not experienced liberty cannot be expected to know what a modern, democratic society looks like, how it functions, or how one goes about building one. Imperfect as it may be, the Cuban Diaspora remains the Cuban nation's most resourceful reservoir of democratic institutional experience. A successful transition in Cuba requires a justice-bound, but non-exclusionary, not-elitist approach to policymaking designed for the rebuilding of the nation. The chapter argues that freedom as the focal point is the only philosophical concept capable of bridging the different sociopolitical and economic values and ideologies that exist in the Cuban nation today.

Chapter VI follows up by discussing how post-Castro Cuba needs to seek sociopolitical and economic policies targeted toward individuals and their fundamental character, not their current dispositions. Post-Castro Cuba will need to rebuild much more than its economy; it will need to rebuild its national identity. A starting point is to recognize fully that Cuba's politico-economic system is not reformable, as in a Darwinian evolutionary process. A philosophy of citizens' empowerment is necessary to begin the return to individual responsibility from the collectivist legacy of Castroism and to recapture individual energies.

Chapter VII focuses on the habitual Cuban contempt for institutional norms and its negative corollaries for effective democratic governance. It reasons that liberal democracy offers the best antidote for the worst anti-institutional aspects of Cuban informality, but only if it is perceived to be convenient and working in the best interest of individual goals. The argument follows that one of the legacies of Castroism is that Cubans will need to be nudged toward decisions that will improve their lives and citizenship and introduces the modern techniques of choice architecture to assist in this endeavor.

Chapter VIII discusses the concept of "happiness" in the context of how the necessary social bonds of trust in people, society, government, etc., are fundamentally absent in Cuba where a distrustful citizenry, unable to survive on the honest product of its labor, routinely engages in illegalities, egoism, untruthfulness, and a general degradation of values. It advances that democracy and well-being are strongly, but not simplistically, linked. It argues for a reform process in Cuba that is broad-based, comprehensive, and carried out expeditiously, as opposed to a program of gradualist reforms.

Part Two builds on the descriptions and analyses of the first eight chapters to reflect on some subject-specific challenges of the reform process that will be faced *mañana* in Cuba: personnel reforms (Chapter IX), institutional reforms (Chapter X), political reforms (Chapter XI), and economic reforms (Chapter XII). The principal objective of these reflections is not to offer detailed, step-by-step reform recommendations, but rather to offer first principles and trenchant observations that may one day serve as a compass to the new generation of leaders who will be responsible for bringing about changes in post-Castro Cuba. It is primarily that new generation of Cubans whom I visualize as my audience while I write these reflections about *mañana* in Cuba. This book is for them, and for all those dissidents who fight valiantly for freedom armed only with their dignity.

Transition scholars agree that no universal prescription exists to deal with the myriad issues involved in rebuilding a country along democratic lines. There are no specific, practical recommendations equally valid for all nations. The emphasis in this work is to offer a current, sociopolitical understanding of the Cuban nation so that Cuban-specific approaches may be undertaken. But the change of systems is above all an autocatalytic political process. The corresponding first principle is that, although expanding the political contour is a necessary condition, the requirements of democracy must take priority and supremacy.

In order to avoid political stasis or chaos in post-Castro Cuba, a new way of perceiving the future and of behaving as a people must emerge. Conflicting political cultures, like scorpions in a bottle, cannot permanently avoid each other. But political cultures, unlike scorpions, need not engage in an elimination fight to the end. They can coexist in a participatory democratic milieu, provided that all participants accept democracy as the field of engagement. For this to happen, however, the transitioning Cuban government cannot be a direct, ideological extension of the Castro regime. Transition in post-Castro Cuba cannot become a more pragmatic mutation of Castroism. It needs to be its antithesis.

This *Mañana in Cuba* vision concludes, in Chapter XIII, as it begins, with the uncompromising idea and defense of freedom. It is a vision that acknowledges the tortuous historical path of the Cuban colonial, republican, and communist experiences and their legacies. But most of all, it is a vision that does not accept Cuba's future as being preordained by its past. To escape its Sisyphean challenge, a successful transition in Cuba will require, perhaps above all else, a compelling vision of hope for all Cubans and an irrefutable revelation that life can regain its potential meaning despite its tragic aspects. It requires a visualization of the future that does not equate the dignity of a society with its economic gains. In post-Castro Cuba, choices will be made and paths will be taken. Let them be those of individual freedoms and empowerment.

Live with the illusion of the return,
but do not think you will return to the illusion.
The sands of time fall inexorably,
and no one returns to his past, or to his youth.
There was a Cuba before you and
there will be a Cuba after you, but
the one you knew and enjoyed
you will never find again.

Luís Aguilar León,
He Aquí que "El Profeta" habla del retorno a Cuba.

Chapter I - Cuba: Alternative Roads in an Uncertain Future

Two roads diverged in a wood, and I,
I took the one less traveled by,
And that has made all the difference

Robert Frost

As the Castro brothers' era comes to an end, for Cubans two roads diverge in an uncertain future. Which one is taken, to paraphrase Robert Frost, will make all the difference. [4] It is an obvious oversimplification to speak of Cuba's future in terms of only two possible paths. There are myriad generic as well as indigenous variations of political and economic systems that may be adopted (and adapted) by any given society. The dichotomy here into just two non-overlapping alternatives is meant to spotlight one path that places individual freedoms and empowerment front-and-center, and another path that does not. One is a governing philosophy that embraces an understanding of human rights and individual freedoms as essential to sustained development; the other advocates the primacy of economic measures, even if undertaken outside the framework of democratic empowerment. One road leads to the advocacy of policies for a rapid democratic transition and the strengthening of civil society and democratic institutions, and

---

4   Frost, Robert. "The Road Not Taken." *Bartleby.com.* 25 January 2009. http://www.bartleby.com/104.67.html

1

the other leads to an indefinite wait before democratic reforms can be instituted.

At the most basic level, two opposed systems of values are at play: one in which primacy goes to human rights, freedoms, and democracy; and one in which priority is given to financial prosperity and economic growth. Understanding the consequences and implications of these alternative paths matters because the path chosen will crystallize the Cuban post-Castro narrative for generations to come.

Cuba today can be described as an impossible country (*un país imposible*), with unsustainable sociopolitical and economic arrangements. For the Cuban people, the experience of more than a half-century of living under a totalitarian regime, and under the constant bombardment of Marxist-Leninist rhetoric, means a legacy of economic, social, political and civil backwardness. This is a continuing legacy of civil society unpreparedness not unlike the one the country faced after the colonial period. Cuba's dysfunctional heritage from a decadent Spain five centuries ago was a significant, perhaps dominant, factor in the post-colonial milieu of corruption and political confusion. Then, Madrid was Cuba's model of political behavior, "a sort of decrepit teacher still living in the past."[5] From Spain's inept political elite, Cubans learned about "bureaucratic corruption, *caudillismo* (warlords), dogmatic intolerance, messianic leadership, a malformed judicial system and a deformed government administration," as well as militarism. [6] These characteristics were evident during the first five decades of the Republic. As eminent Cuban historian and professor Jaime Suchlicki points out:

> By the time of Chibás' death [in 1951], Cuba's political life was a sad spectacle ... Politics came to be regarded by the Cuban people with disrespect. To become a politician was to enter into an elite, a new class apart from the interest of the people. The elected politicians did not owe allegiances

---

5   Roig, Pedro. *Death of a Dream: History of Cuba* . Miami: Rodes Press, 2008: 174

6   Ibid. p. 174

to their constituencies, not even to their nation, but only to
themselves ... Political figures furthermore were the objects
of popular mockery. [7]

Today, the Castro brothers' decadent politico-economic system
bequeaths Cubans the same inheritance of a civil society unprepared
for the demands of a liberal democracy and a competitive market
economy. Today, as in 1902, Cuba's unfortunate political heritage
foretells of enormous difficulties in the years ahead. For many in Cuba,
the political ideology they have been taught for fifty years represents
their primary frame of reference.

Over seventy-three percent of the Cuban population was born in the
revolutionary period after 1959.[8] As a practical matter, only retirement-
age Cubans can have any adult recollection of enjoying individual
freedoms. Stated differently, no Cuban under the age of fifty has lived
with a free press, free labor unions, or an independent judicial system
or legislature; nor has he participated in pluralistic elections or in any
way been exposed to the rights, privileges, and obligations of citizens in
a pluralistic democratic system. In 1902, in his inauguration as Cuba's
first president, Don Tomás Estrada Palma is said to have noted, "We
finally have a republic; now we need citizens."[9] A great tragedy of the
Cuban experience is that over a century after independence from Spain,
post-Castro Cuba still faces the same paucity of responsible citizenship
behavioral patterns.

But conceptually, the term "unprepared" masks a deeper, more
pernicious, and fundamental characteristic of the Cuban sociopolitical
psyche. That is a lack of appreciation, perhaps even contempt, for the
vicissitudes of democratic institutions and governance. Hand-in-hand

---

7   Suchlicki, Jaime. *Cuba: From Columbus to Castro and Beyond.* Washington,
    D.C.: Brassey's, INC, 2000: 115

8   Kollbrunner, Marcus. "50 Years since the Cuban Revolution." *China Worker.*
    11 January 2009. London. 20 January 2009. Chinaworker.org/en/content/
    news/608/

9   Gutiérrez-Boronat, Orlando. *La República Invisible.* Rodes Printing: 123

with this contempt for institutions goes a historical belief in violence as a legitimate means through which to achieve political objectives.

Notwithstanding the sad spectacle of its political life, at the time of Fidel Castro's revolution, Cuba enjoyed one of the highest standards of living in Latin America, with a growing, well-educated middle class. As it were, the generation of Cuban adults that welcomed Castro's ascension to power was the most democratically experienced generation in Cuba's history following the 1940 Constitution and the constitutionally freely elected presidents (1940–1952). No other Cuban generation before or since has had more exposure to democratic governance or institutions. And yet, this generation—Cuba's most prepared in terms of democratic values, consciousness and civil responsibilities—acquiesced overtly to the dismantling of due process and the rule of law.

In February 1959, just one month into the revolution, Fidel Castro transferred all legislative powers to his "Council of Ministers" in a blatant violation of the constitution he had vowed to uphold. Cubans applauded. When José Miro Cardona, a highly respected attorney serving as the provisional government's Prime Minister, resigned in protest, Cubans responded with a collective yawn. The following month, when a revolutionary tribunal acquitted a group of Batista's air force personnel of war crimes, Fidel Castro was infuriated by the acquittal and ordered a new trial, in which the accused were dutifully found guilty. Explaining his action, Castro stated that "revolutionary justice is based not on legal precepts but on moral convictions." As historian and attorney Pedro Roig points out, "If that was a valid premise, the question was then: whose moral convictions?"[10] Once again, Cubans failed to protest the manifest trampling of due process and the rule of law.

These and many other early 1959 attacks on democratic values and institutions were not covert, marginal, or disputed controversial violations. They were an open and flagrant abandonment of core democratic institutional values and precepts. Each case was met with indifference and perhaps even complicity by the majority of Cubans. The tragic paradox is that throughout their history, Cubans have

---

10 Roig, op. cit., 288

fought persistently and valiantly for independence, for social justice, and more abstractly for the Motherland. However, political rights and civil liberties, and just as critically their supporting institutions, have not ignited comparable patriotic fervor.

Sadly, the last five decades of totalitarian rule have further distanced the Cuban population from an understanding and robust appreciation for the role of democratic institutions and civil society. In the Cuban political mindset, messianic leadership trumps democratic institutions every time.

Change in Cuba: How Citizens View Their Country's Future[11]

In 2008, Freedom House conducted in-depth interviews with a cross-section of Cuban citizens in five Cuban provinces. The research explored how citizens view their country's future. These interviews allow us a glimpse into the contemporary attitudes and mores of Cuban civil society. According to the Freedom House report, young Cubans, while particularly disillusioned, are mostly politically apathetic. For them, as for most Cubans, the emblematic response to government injustice is to complain and conform. This dreary attitude has developed over decades of government intimidation and indoctrination. One respondent further explained the cynicism and apathy as "*cambiar para que todo siga igual*" ("change so that everything stays the same").[12]

A key research finding is that for Cubans on the island, the major concerns relate to bread-and-butter issues. "Outside of economic concerns, few respondents named political issues as cause for concern. Only artists and intellectuals were concerned with the lack of civil and

---

11 "Change in Cuba: How Citizens View Their Country's Future." *Freedom House.* Special Report. 15 September 2008. http://www.freedomhouse.org/uploads/ ChangeinCuba.pdf

12 Ibid., p. 10

political rights."[13] This is not surprising, given Cuba's abysmal economic situation. But when asked what they would do if reforms do not take place within the next few years, the answer was "nothing." Interviewees also expressed that if they could no longer conform, they would seek to leave the country. Another significant finding of the Freedom House research is that although Cuban youth are the most disillusioned segment of the population, they are also apathetic to political issues and do not see themselves as capable of organizing a movement for change. Significantly, all but one of the respondents under age thirty expressed a desire to leave the country.

This political apathy, or perhaps capitulation, particularly within the dissatisfied youth, stands in sharp contrast with the historical political activism of Cuba's student movements, particularly from the 1930s to the early years of the revolution. If changing mores capture the fundamental values of society, it seems that conforming has taken root in Cuba's society. In Cuba, the psychological fight-or-flight stress response has been reformulated to conform-or-flight.

Based on the responses to questions regarding the activities of pro-democracy dissident groups, Cubans appear unwilling to participate. "When asked about the possibility of a public protest, many respondents were perplexed and did not know how to answer."[14] Cubans today view action against the authorities as ineffective and dangerous, and discount the possibility that a popular response could lead to political change; rather, emigration is viewed as the ultimate form of protest, with quiet acceptance as the second option.

In terms of the future, the Freedom House report finds that Cubans perceive civil society as thin and irrelevant. They believe change can only take place from the top down—from within the Communist Party. To Cubans, change from the bottom up, originating with civil society, is inconceivable.

Also in 2008, a Cuban Public Opinion Survey was undertaken by The International Republican Institute (IRI). [15] Personal face-to-

---

13   Ibid., p. 3

14   Ibid., p.20

15   "Cuban Public Opinion Survey." *The International Republican Institute.* 20 June

face interviews employing a stratified-intercept methodology were conducted with Cuban adults in all fourteen Cuban provinces. For current purposes, one of the most telling questions was: "What do you think is the biggest problem in Cuba?" Aggregately, only 8.9 percent of the respondents cited "Lack of Freedoms/Political System" as the biggest problem. As in the Freedom House interviews, bread-and-butter issues dominated the concerns. For example, aggregately the main concerns for 56.9 percent of respondents were Low Salaries/High Cost of Living, together with the Double Currency Standard.

Other specified concerns were: Embargo/Isolation 8.5%, Food Scarcity 6.8 %, Health/Lack of Medicine 4.3 %, Poor Transportation Infrastructure 4.1%, Lack of or Dilapidated Housing 2.4%. The age distribution of the top three responses shows that the overwhelming concern with bread-and-butter issues over lack of freedoms is consistent across the age brackets.

"What do you think is the biggest problem in Cuba?"		
	Low Salaries / High Cost of Living / And Double Currency System	Lack of Freedoms / Political System
18 – 29 years old	60.8 %	11.2 %
30 – 39 years old	66.7 %	11.8 %
40 – 49 years old	57.0 %	13.2%
50 – 59 years old	52.8 %	5.6%
Older than 60	43.5 %	0.9%

2008. http://www.iri.org/lac/cuba/pdfs/2008%20June%205%20Survey%20of%20Cuban%20Public%20Opinion,%20March%2014-April%2012,%202008.pdf

Perhaps it is possible to explain this feeble concern with civil liberties and political rights in psychological Maslovian terms by noting that Cubans must dedicate an inordinately large portion of their daily lives to the tasks associated with meeting the most basic physiological needs.[16] According to Maslow's "hierarchy of needs" thesis, higher-level needs only come into focus once the lower-level needs are met. If Cubans must dedicate most of their day to making ends meet (*resolviendo,* or resolving), they cannot, or so the argument goes, think about the more abstract, higher-level, "self-actualization" (in Maslow's terminology) needs. Some researchers, however, have found little evidence for the hierarchical structure of needs proposed by Maslow, and others note that fundamental human needs are non-hierarchical and are ontologically universal. That is, needs are invariant in nature and simply a condition of being human.

Clearly, when people's physical and mental energies are totally directed to daily survival, there is little left for less immediate needs. In a totalitarian state such as Cuba, daily survival includes avoiding arbitrary imprisonment or the loss of one's job. Preoccupation with basic survival needs is a force mitigating against political activism. But in the Cuban context, this theoretical construct does not explain apathy toward lack of civil liberties, particularly in the youth. As noted earlier, the current political apathy stands in sharp contrast to the historical political activism of Cuba's student movements and their struggle for the higher-level needs of truth and justice.

A mid-2006 Gallup poll conducted with six hundred Havana residents and four hundred Santiago residents showed that only one in four Cuban respondents (26 percent) were satisfied with their freedom to choose what to do with their lives—the lowest satisfaction figure in the Gallup database of more than one hundred countries, and much lower than the 79 percent satisfaction across urban centers in twenty Latin America countries.[17] It seems that in Cuba today there is an

---

16 Abraham Harold Maslow (April 1, 1908–June 8, 1970), American psychologist. He is noted for his conceptualization of a "hierarchy of needs," and is considered the father of humanistic psychology.

17 Gallup. "Just One in Four Urban Cubans Satisfied with Personal Freedoms."

intellectual disconnect between the very personal question regarding the freedom to choose what do to with one's life and the more abstract constructs of civil liberties, political rights, and the Communist system. Although Cubans may want more personal freedoms, the majority of respondents to the Gallup poll—having been born since 1959—appear to have internalized the socialist values of the regime. This internalization of socialist values is perhaps a better explanation for the contrast between the current political apathy and the historical political activism of Cuba's student movements and their idealistic struggles for truth and justice.

In some imperfect sense, this internalization of socialist values can be thought of as analogous to the psychological response sometimes seen in abducted hostages, where the victims become emotionally attached to their captors, a sort of collective Cuban "Stockholm syndrome."[18] One psychological explanation of Stockholm syndrome is that of cognitive dissonance. In essence, people do not like feeling unhappy for extended periods. As captives, they would be constantly unhappy, unless they resolved the cognitive dissonance by learning to identify with their captors. Stockholm syndrome captives find ways of sympathizing with their captors by believing, for instance, that the captors may be showing them favor with small acts of kindness. Captives fail to recognize fully the self-serving nature of the captor's actions. The Cuban Communist system has for decades used mechanisms such as the *"Tarjeta de Abastecimiento,"* a food ration card astutely and machiavellianly misnamed as a supply card, to profess the benevolence of the state in providing for the citizenry. The ration card is, of course, a camouflaged state control mechanism that promotes identification with, and dependence on, the state.

To frame and conceptualize this internalization of socialist values phenomenon, it is also helpful to sketch below some of the articles

---

December 2006. http://www.gallup.com/poll/25915/just-one-four-urban-cubans-satisfied-personal-freedoms.aspx

18 The term was coined by psychiatrist Nils Bejerot, who assisted police in the famed Kreditbanken robbery in Stockholm, in which the bank robbers held bank employees hostage for six days in 1973.

of the Cuban Penal Code used to suppress dissent. These are articles repugnant to our democratic principles, but codified in socialist law:

> Article 144 defines the crime of *desacato,* or "disrespect"
>
> Articles 208 and 209 define the crime of *asociación ilícita,* or "illicit association"
>
> Article 103 defines the crime of *propaganda enemiga,* or "enemy propaganda"
>
> Article 207 defines the crime of *asociación para delinquir,* or "associating with others to commit crimes"
>
> Article 115 defines the crime of *difusión de falsas informaciones contra la paz internacional,* or "dissemination of false information against international peace"
>
> Article 143 defines the crime of *resistencia o desobediencia,* or "resistance or disobedience"
>
> Articles 72–90 define the crime of *peligrosidad,* or "social dangerousness"

These articles broadly define disrespect, illicit association, disobedience, dangerousness, etc., in terms of acting in a manner that contradicts "socialist morality" or engaging in "anti-social behavior." Notwithstanding our revulsion at these infringements to civil liberties and political rights, these articles reflect the socialist values that Cubans have lived under for decades. The conceptualization as a crime of social dangerousness is particularly pernicious because it imprisons people for illegal activities they are predisposed to commit in the future, a real-life *Minority Report* of sorts. [19]

---

19 The film directed by Stephen Spielberg is about a future society where murders are prevented through the efforts of three mutants who can see the future. The story mainly concerns the paradoxes and alternate realities that are created by the precognition of crimes when the chief of police intercepts a precognition that he is about to murder a man he has never met.

And yet, in a 2009 analytical work titled "Crisis over Crisis," Cuban economist and dissident Oscar Espinosa Chepe writes from Havana of the impact of Cuba's economic situation on civil society: "These years of prolonged and deep crisis have generated an enormous loss of spiritual values in large segments of the population. Egoism, mendacity, double morality, and all illegal methods of survival have proliferated to incredible levels." Cuban children, Espinosa Chepe tells us, grow up witnessing how their parents, obligated by circumstances, live by theft and illegality. Since Cubans cannot live by the results of their legitimate labors, and work has ceased to be the principal source of one's livelihood, a quasi-ethic has evolved that justifies everything.[20]

No Revolution of Rising Expectations

In 1962, American sociologist James C. Davies sought to explain revolutionary movements in terms of rising individual expectations and falling levels of perceived well-being.[21] According to Davies, violent civil disturbances that cause the displacement of one ruling group by another are most likely to occur when a prolonged period of economic and social development is followed by a short period of sharp reversal. In Davies's argumentation, the actual level of socio-economic development is less significant than the expectation that past progress can continue. With the benefit of hindsight, Davies's theory may offer a partial explanation to the somewhat paradoxical success of Castro's revolution at a time when Cuba had achieved one of the highest levels of economic and social development in Latin America.

For Davies, political stability and instability are ultimately dependent on a state of mind, a mood in society. It is the state of mind or mood rather than the actual availability of material or psychological goods that brings about instability. In the case of Cuba

---

20 Espinosa Chepe, Oscar. "Crisis Sobre Crisis." XIX Conferencia de la Asociacion para el Estudio de la Economía Cubana. 2009. Author's translation

21 James C. Davies, "Toward a Theory of Revolution." *American Sociological Review,* 27.1 (1962): 5-19.

today, fifty years of totalitarian rule have engendered a rare static state of very low human aspirations—a social, political and economic stasis of conformism. Enduring hardships, lack of freedoms, and constant preoccupations with physical survival have coalesced into mute despair and a withdrawal from any activity unrelated to making ends meet. In short, the collective and sustained despair induced by Castro's rule does not meet Davies's criteria of a sudden reversal in fortunes following a sustained period of economic growth.

The accuracy and therefore the utility of interviews and public opinion surveys conducted under repressive totalitarian conditions are often problematic. In addition to the interviews and public opinion surveys discussed above, we can also look at actions to help us assess the collective Cuban mood. The state of mind of Cubans is one of conform-or-flight, as evidenced by the nearly two million Cubans that have fled the island and the millions more that would leave if that option were available. Approximately one out of six Cubans has chosen to live outside the country. As Alexis de Tocqueville noted in discussing the French Revolution, "Evils which are patiently endured when they seem inevitable become intolerable when the idea of escape from them is suggested."[22]

In Cuba, another form of escape from hopelessness and existential angst is suicide. Cuba's suicide rate of 12.4 per 100,000 inhabitants in 2005 was the highest in Latin America.[23] The suicide rate reached a high of 21.3 per 100,000 in 1992. These figures do not take into account the thousands of Cuban rafters that have died in the Florida Straits in what can be considered near-suicidal attempts to escape the island. The historical significance and interpretation of the practice of suicide in Cuba's culture lies outside our present focus. "For more than 150 years, the rate of suicide in Cuba has ranked consistently among the highest in the world. It has long been the highest in all of Latin

---

22 A. de Tocqueville, *The Old Regime and the French Revolution* (trans.by John Bonner), N.Y.: Harper & Bros., 1856: 214. As quoted by James C. Davies.

23 World Health Organization. "Suicide Rates in Cuba, 1963–2005." Suicide Prevention and Special Programmes. 24 January 2009. http://www.who.int/mental_health/media/cuba.pdf

America."[24] But as Cuban historian Louis A. Perez explains in *To Die in Cuba - Suicide and Society*, it is not always discernible if suicide originates with internal or external causes, "but neither is it possible to separate the psychology of self-destruction from the sociology of suicide." [25]

In the context of the incoherence of life in Cuba, suicide as taking to the seas and living in exile may be viewed as exercises in political self-determination. The decision to take one's life makes a judgment on one's view of the future. It is a statement of what can be expected from life. The future is all about possibilities, but Cubans must surely wonder, "What good is the future if you die before it arrives?"[26] After fifty years of economic hardships and political repression, it is difficult to view them as temporary conditions. The circumstances that drive individuals to suicide offer insights into their expectations of life.

In his classic essay "The Myth of Sisyphus," Albert Camus introduces his philosophy of the absurd; of man's search for meaning in an unintelligible world devoid of God and eternal truths and values. He questions if the realization of meaninglessness and absurdity in one's life necessarily requires suicide. He concludes that it does not, but that the absurd can never be accepted. In Camus' view, the absurd requires confrontation and revolt, and the "absurd man" should live as if "everything is permitted"—no ethical rules apply. Without a meaning in life, there can be no values. This is the quasi-ethic that has developed in Cuba's civil society, which justifies everything as described above by Oscar Espinosa Chepe. Cuba's civil society has committed a sort of philosophical and ethical suicide to escape the existential absurdity of a future without possibilities.

To speak coherently of *mañana* in Cuba, it is necessary not only to understand the historical context of current attitudes and values, but also to analyze them with an eye to social development principles.

---

24 Perez Jr., Louis A. *To Die in Cuba, Suicide and Society*. Chapell Hill. Thee University of North Carolina Press. 2005: 5

25 Ibid., p 8.

26 As the character Adela does in the play *Donde está la luz*, by Ramon Ferreira as quoted in Louis A. Perez in *To Die in Cuba*, p. 16.

Putting aside our limited understanding of fundamental social processes, they function, with other factors, as enabling conditions. When thinking about Cuba's future, there is a strong tendency to focus on the instruments of transition: social policies, economic programs, investments and capital, institution-building, and more. But the ultimate determinant of Cuba's transitional developmental path will not be the instruments themselves, since they do not exist independently of society. Ultimately, effectiveness resides with the society that employs the instruments rather than the instruments themselves.[27]

In other words, Cuba's future is more a function of national aspirations, attitudes, values, and the corresponding choices that will be made by Cuban society. And therein lies a core problem, given the current collective Cuban state of mind. Achievements in the transition process of the Cuba of tomorrow will flow from intangible social attitudes that are not prevalent today, such as confidence in the government, trust in other people, tolerance, and cooperation. As noted by Jacobs and Cleveland, "Values are central organizing principles or ideas that govern and determine human behavior." Values give direction to our thought processes, sentiments, emotional energies, preferences, and actions.[28]

Cubans today do not venture to dream or hope, except perhaps about leaving the island. They do not exhibit rising expectations particularly in terms of aspirations for self-determination, civil liberties, and political rights. Expectations rise when liberties and rights are democratically protected, and Cubans have not enjoyed democratically protected liberties and rights for several generations.

A successful transition in Cuba will require a new set of values based on self-confidence, self-reliance, courage to fight for one's rights, greater social tolerance and social equality, reconciliation, and aspiration for higher accomplishments. The goals a society strives for are influenced not just by needs, but also by values. Values represent the most effective

---

27 Jacobs, Garry and Cleveland, Harland. "Social Development Theory." International Center for Peace and Development (ICPD), November 1, 1999. The discussion that follows borrows liberally from this work.

28 Ibid.

and efficient form of organization for channeling human energies in constructive and productive ways. But the values that can be observed in Cuba today are not compatible with the behaviors most conducive to propelling a reluctant population to imagine itself as a free nation and to aspire to that status.

The present-day hopelessness of Cuban civil society is poignantly captured by prominent Cuban blogger Yoani Sánchez, whose blog *Generación Y* reveals much about sociopolitical realities in Cuba. In Yoani's words, "Most young people's eyes are looking to the outside, because they see that they cannot make change in their country. They only see the status quo. Most young people desire to take a plane to Miami or Europe and in 10 hours change their lives completely. They know they cannot realize their dreams here."

This is not an auspicious set of sociopolitical attitudes for *mañana* in Cuba.

Chapter II – Freedom from Fear

It is not power that corrupts but fear.
Fear of losing power corrupts those who
wield it, and fear of the scourge of power
corrupts those who are subject to it.

Aung San Suu Kyi

A DEFINING FEATURE OF THE Cuban experience under Castro has been repression and the concomitant destruction of anything resembling an independent civil society. "Cuba has been characterized by an intrusive state whose elites have atomized society, controlled and reorganized it, and channeled participation vertically through a host of [government-based] mass organizations. This process has eliminated political competition, destroyed economic society, and rendered civil society weak and ineffective."[29] Cuban civil society has been distanced from democratic values and institutions by five decades of isolationism. For five decades, fear has been an integral part of the everyday Cuban existence.

In a system that denies basic freedoms, society is debilitated and corrupted by a miasma of fear. As 1991 Nobel Peace Prize laureate, human-rights activist, and prisoner of conscience Aung San Suu Kyi maintains, "It is not power that corrupts, but fear." The effects of fear

---

29   Mujal-León, Eusebio. "Can Cuba Change? Tensions in the Regime." *Journal of Democracy.* 20, 1. January 2009: 20-35.

are pervasive throughout society; fear corrupts those who exert it and those who are subject to it. "With so close a relationship between fear and corruption, it is little wonder that in any society where fear is rife, corruption in all forms becomes deeply entrenched ... A people who would build a nation in which strong, democratic institutions are firmly established as a guarantee against state-induced power must first learn to liberate their own minds from apathy and fear."[30]

In this framework, the apathetic behavior exhibited by today's Cuban society, as discussed in the last chapter, may be viewed as a most sinister form of fear. It is a fear that masquerades as common sense, or even wisdom. It is a fear that condemns as foolish, reckless, or futile the small daily acts of courage of Cuban dissidents. It is a fear that must be conquered if any national project of transition is to stand a chance of success. "Among the basic freedoms to which men aspire ... freedom from fear stands out as both a means and an end."[31] The observation that freedom from fear works as both a means and an end is replete with insights for policy formulation.

Much has been said here and elsewhere about the enormous challenges to genuine democratic governance intrinsic in the Cuban civic values experience. Professor Damian J. Fernandez argues that "promoting a civil democratic culture will be the greatest challenge that the Cuban people ... will confront in a post-transition Cuba."[32] Indeed; moreover, there must first exist an intellectual conviction of the need to embrace the mental attitudes, values, and institutions that promote a nation's development. The success of national policies is contingent on the willing participation of the people. In a nutshell, "Cubans seem to want to be free from politics rather than agents of it, while holding at the same time high expectations of what the state should deliver."[33]

Initiatives which seek to alter primarily official policies and mechanisms to improve economic and material conditions have little

---

30 Aung San Suu Kyi. *Freedom from Fear*. New York. Penguin Books. 1995: 181

31 Ibid., p.183

32 Fernandez, Damian J. "The Greatest Challenges: Civic Values in Post-Transition Cuba." *Cuba Transition Project*. 2003: 1

33 Ibid., p. ii

chance of sustained success. There is much in current (and historical) Cuban values, attitudes, and behavioral patterns that does not offer fertile ground for liberal democratic governance. It is also true that the tenet that values and culture can be altered with the right policy prescriptions is highly questionable. Social engineering, as Fernandez points out, is a "monumental proposition at best, whose record in terms of U.S. policy initiatives and outcomes is mixed even in the most optimistic of assessments."[34] This challenge must be approached and treated not in terms of social engineering, but as part of an unending enterprise to show that a society can transcend its detracting characteristics and features.

At its core, democracy is a political system that proposes to empower individuals. The proposition that people should be sufficiently empowered to participate meaningfully in the governance of their country is anathema to the Cuban governing elite, who believe Cubans are not suited to enjoy the rights and privileges of democratic citizenship. The self-serving corollary of this belief is that the governing elite itself is entitled to more rights and privileges than those afforded by democratic governance; thus the unsuitability of liberal democracy for Cuban society. This is, of course, an abhorrent, vacuous argument, but one that needs to be addressed in light of Cuban anti-institutionalism and the manifest decay in democratic civil values we have been discussing.

Freedom from fear is the first step for a genuine and successful transition, because it is a necessary condition to reversing political apathy. Václav Havel says of his first becoming a political activist, "I stopped waiting for the world to improve and exercised my right to intervene in that world, or at least to express my opinion about it."[35] For a society, freedom from fear requires living in an integrated social and ideological system based on respect for the individual. In Cuba, it requires not just a change in government or economic policies, but a change in sociopolitical values. It requires what Aung San Suu Kyi calls a revolution of the spirit. "Feel always free," she exhorts. "We need to

---

34 Ibid., p.16

35 Aung San Suu Kyi. *The Voice of Hope*. New York. Seven Stories Press. 2008: 7

remember this … Feel always free." Cubans have forgotten how to feel free.

The "China Model" Syndrome

The view that economic progress is an essential antecedent to civic empowerment and the counterargument that civic empowerment is the foundation of progress may seem to differ only in terms of the sequencing and prioritizing of policies. However, the differences are philosophically fundamental. The first looks to economic measures as the key to unlocking human worth. The second sees individual freedoms and empowerment as essential to living meaningful lives.

In addition, there seems to be a working expectation that improvements in material conditions usher in democratic governance. Often, improving Cuba's economy and the material well-being of its population is offered, not as an end in itself, but as a step in a process of raising expectations that leads predictably to freedoms and democratic empowerments. As an empirical proposition, this thesis is demonstrably false. As a logical argument the hypothesis that economic improvements *ex ante* democratic reforms are a legitimate path to freedoms contains logical "false cause" fallacies of the chicken-and-egg variety inversing cause and effect relationships. The core principle of this variant is that changes in the economic sphere lead to changes in the political one. But material yardsticks alone are not adequate indicators of human well-being or of the mental comforts that give dignity to human existence. Neither can it be assumed that material progress causes improvements in social, political or ethical standards.

Let's explore this persistent argument that if a country achieves economic success, all else will follow using the tool kit of logic or critical thinking. Supporters of this view often point to China and Vietnam as two countries that have embraced, albeit selectively, a market economy. They note correctly that these countries have shown remarkable economic growth and that their peoples are measurably wealthier. But the argument begins to falter when we cannot find the expected and anticipated political reforms in the direction of democracy. Without evidence of democratic reforms in these countries, any argument by analogy fails. Arguably, democracy may still follow, but it is now legitimate to ask: When? And what empirical support is offered for this claim? Technically, the proposition may be said to contain a classical "appeal to ignorance" (*ad ignorantiam*) fallacy arguing that the democracy claim is valid because it may still come to pass. Even if someday China and Vietnam were to embrace democratic reforms, no causation can be legitimately postulated on the basis of mere succession in time—an "after this, therefore because of this" logical fallacy. Correlation does not prove causation.

The empirical case against this argument is unequivocal, as can be shown by taking a detailed timeline look at China and Vietnam in terms of political rights and civil liberties over a thirty-four-year time period.[36] Quantitative measures of political rights and civil liberties have been compiled yearly since 1972 by Freedom House in their "Freedom in the World" series of country ratings. Freedom House measures sub-categories for political rights to include a.) Electoral processes, b.) Political pluralism and participation and, c.) Functioning of government. For civil liberties, the sub-categories measure a.) Freedom of expression and belief, b.) Association and organizational rights, c.) Rule of law, and d.) Personal autonomy and individual rights. To measure political rights and civil liberties, Freedom House uses a one-to-seven scale, with one representing the highest degree of freedoms and seven the lowest.

The empirical measures show no improvement in political rights in China in the thirty-four-year time period. China rated a seven (worst) in 1972 and still rates at that level today. Notwithstanding all the economic changes that have taken place over this time period, they have not caused the Chinese leadership to usher in any improvements in political rights. An almost identical situation has occurred with respect to civil liberties. China shows a zigzag pattern from seven (worst) to six

---

36   A more comprehensive analysis can be found in: Azel, José. "How to Think about Change in Cuba: A guide for Policymakers." *Cuban Affairs Electronic Journal*. 3.3 September 2008.

and one half for a few years, then back to seven, and currently sits at six and one half. In the end, China's best measured level of civil liberties, first recorded in 1977, is the same thirty years later. China's zigzag civil liberties pattern serves to illustrate another issue: the reversibility of even minor gains in civil liberties in the absence of democratic governance and institutions. This underscores that a government accountable to the people is the best defense for civil liberties.

For Vietnam, the data show essentially the same patterns: no improvements whatsoever in political rights, and only very recent and minor improvements in civil liberties. The cases of China and Vietnam demonstrate that no empirical case can be made in support of the hypothesis that economic reforms lead inexorably, linearly, or on a timely basis to political reforms. The evidence strongly suggests that they do not. Even so, the empirical evidence alone does not allow the conclusion that economic changes will never lead to political reforms. As philosophers and logicians will be quick to point out, the rules of formal argumentation state that failure to uncover tenable reasons for affirming that economic changes lead to political reforms does not mean that the hypothesis is disproved. Failure to find such evidence concerns only the reasonableness of such belief. Theoretically, a hard-to-predict and rare event beyond the realm of normal expectations could occur—a black swan event.[37] But why support a path that relies on the imponderable, sacrificing individual freedoms in the process?

---

37 The term *black swan* originates with the ancient Western conception that all swans are white. In that context, a black swan was a metaphor for something that could not exist. The seventeenth-century discovery of black swans in Australia broadened the term to connote that a perceived impossibility could actually come to pass.

Economic Changes sans Political Changes: Where Do They Lead?

The section above refuted the causal argument that economic reforms lead predictably to freedoms and democratic empowerments. However, the instinct to opt for narrowly focused short-term economic benefits may be more modest in scope and respond only to a minimalist desire to improve the material well-being of the Cuban people. This version of the argument concedes that there is no evidence that improvements in material conditions usher in democratic governance. Nonetheless, it advocates economic reforms on humanitarian grounds even in the absence of freedoms, and more disquieting, even if it may delay the advent of freedoms. The moral and ethical dimensions of this position are complex and troubling. In and of itself, improving the material well-being of peoples is a laudable objective. One worrying aspect is that of harmful consequences. "If material betterment, which is but a means to human happiness, is sought in ways that wound the human spirit, it can in the long run lead to greater human suffering."[38] There is also a dimension of questionable efficacy. "The vast possibilities that a market economy can open up to developing countries can be realized only if economic reforms are undertaken within a framework that recognizes human needs."[39] We can also explore other considerations for rejecting this narrow focus on material benefits.

In *Russia's Capitalist Revolution*, Anders Aslund, an expert in "transition economics," explores why market reforms succeeded in Russia while the building of democracy failed. He notes that when Mikhail Gorbachev was first elected General Secretary of the Communist Party of the Soviet Union, he saw the shortcomings of the Soviet system but "wanted to reform the system to make it better, refusing to draw the logical conclusion to abandon communism."[40] Boris Yeltsin in turn also concentrated on economic reform and left political reforms for later. In

---

38 Aung San Suu Kyi, *Freedom from Fear,* pp. 267

39 Ibid., pp.267

40 Aslund, Anders. *Russia's Capitalist Revolution.* Washington D.C. Peterson Institute for International Economics. 2007: 80.

Russia, the dominant reform idea was economic reform. As a result, in Russia today, civil society is inarticulate and incapable of holding rulers accountable. Aslund concluded, "The short explanation of why market reforms succeeded in Russia, while democracy failed, is that the initial big bang of radical [economic] reforms was sufficient, while democratic reforms were never designed."[41] The Russian experience, among others, shows that no modern society can function in the best interest of the people without an effective system of checks and balances. Not only did democracy fail, but the success of market reforms needs to be qualified as predatory.

The Russian interregnum experience offers interesting parallels that should be kept in mind when thinking about *mañana* in Cuba. If the dominant reform idea is confined to the economics domain and not sociopolitical, with individual freedoms and empowerment front-and-center, the best case scenario may be a low-quality democracy (if it can be called that) similar to the Russian experience. The role of the Cuban military in the economy has been extensive and pervasive. By some estimates, the military management elite control over sixty percent of the economy. Analogously to the Russian experience, where former KGB officers and other officials benefited inordinately from economic reforms, Cuban generals may metamorphose into businessmen.

In a system where enterprises are state owned and managed, the military officers turned businessmen enjoy the privileges of an elite ruling class. Their standard of living is higher, they move into better homes, and the like. But these benefits are miniscule when compared with the opportunities to gain significant wealth by acquiring an equity ownership position in the enterprises under their managerial control. In other words, managing government-owned enterprises offers only limited benefits; owning the enterprise is a far more rewarding and lucrative option.

In tomorrow's Cuba, the enterprise managing military elite will be highly motivated to lead the way towards a privatization of the economy in order to gain the monetary benefits of ownership. A "liberalization" of the Cuban economy following its militarization under Communism,

---

41 Ibid., p. 296

if not conducted in a transparent democratic environment, is likely to make the military elite into instant millionaires as the new Cuban "captains of industry." In the Russian experience, only sixteen years after the collapse of the Soviet Union, we learned that "Russia with 87 billionaires is the new number two country behind the U.S., easily overtaking Germany, with 59 billionaires."[42] Either Russian businessmen possess the most extraordinary entrepreneurial skills in world history, or their ascendancy in wealth accumulation has a suspect origin. In his book, Aslund quotes a Russian oligarch telling him, "There are three kinds of businessmen in Russia. One group is murderers. Another group steals from private individuals. And then you have honest businessmen like us who only steal from the state."[43]

The Cuban population may not view these ownership changes as particularly undesirable or nefarious. They may even welcome them as a positive transition toward free markets and prosperity. In this disheartening end-game scenario, Cuban communism comes to an end, leaving generals, devoid of a democratic culture, as the *nouveau riche*. Putative economic reforms conducted without the individual freedoms and citizenship empowerment of hand-in-hand political reforms will lead to a massive transfer of wealth from the state to a military/party elite. If the dominant concept of reform is limited to economic changes, the result is likely to be, as in Russia, a government focused on extending the personal wealth of the mandarins at the expense of the population, or what political scientists call a kleptocracy.

In the end, the argument for material betterment at the cost of individual freedoms, as Aung San Suu Kyi wrote, "in ways that wound the human spirit," is not defensible if other paths are available—and they are. In contrast to China, Vietnam, and Russia, other former communist countries followed a different course and are today both more prosperous and democratic. The Czech Republic and Estonia, for example introduced democratic reforms emphasizing political

---

42 Kroll, Luisa. "The World's Billionaires 2008." *Forbes*. 5 March 2008. http://www.forbes.com/lists/2008/03/05/richest-people-billionaires-billionaires08-cx_lk_0305billie_land.html.

43 Åslund, Anders. *Russia's Capitalist Revolution*. pp. 160

rights and civil liberties from the beginning of their transition process with outstanding results. If the evidence shows that the most successful transitioning countries have embraced democracy prior to or simultaneously with economic reforms, what case can be made for not insisting on individual freedoms and empowerment?

In 1989, Czechoslovakia embraced political rights decisively in its Velvet revolution. By 1993, the new Czech Republic had transitioned from a seven (worst) in the Freedom House measures discussed earlier to a one (best). Just as revealing is the fact that by 2006, according to the World Bank, the country became the first former member of the Council for Mutual Economic Assistance (COMECON) to achieve developed country status. Compared to the former COMECON countries, the Czech Republic also rates best in the Human Development Index.[44] The country also moved resolutely in 1989 to assure the civil rights of its population and is currently at the highest level of one.

Similarly, Estonia, since regaining its independence in 1991, moved quickly with hand-in-hand structural economic and political reforms. Today, the country is rated one in both political rights and civil liberties. On the economic side, Estonia's market reforms place it among the economic leaders of the former COMECON countries. Today, the country is recognized for its economic freedom, with a balanced budget, almost non-existent public debt, flat-rate income tax, free-trade regime, fully convertible currency, hospitable environment for foreign investment, and more.

The failure of economic reforms to propel individual freedoms in countries like China and Vietnam, taken together with the successes brought about by empowering citizens in examples like the Czech Republic and Estonia, make a strong case for the path that places individual freedoms and empowerment front and center.

---

44 The Human Development Index (HDI) is an index combining normalized measures of life expectancy, literacy, education, and GDP per capita for countries worldwide. It is claimed a standard means of measuring human development, a concept that, according to the United Nations Development Program (UNDP) refers to the process of widening the options of persons, giving them greater opportunities for education, health care, income, employment, etc

A related argument that is often made in favor of a very gradual approach to change is that such a gradualist approach is necessary to avoid the possible chaos resulting from more comprehensive and rapid changes. It is argued that Cuba's abysmal set of initial sociopolitical and economic conditions is such that the introduction of comprehensive massive changes could result in a failed state.

The main concern hinges on the precarious balance between openness in a society and stability in that society. It is certainly the case that economic reforms—particularly reforms to begin a transition from a command economy to a market economy—are destabilizing. Decollectivization and desocialization create enormous social dislocations. They require a repositioning of the role of the state and a new model of social relationships between the state and its people. Whatever the specific strategies selected, they will demand many difficult choices.

As Ian Bremmer points out in *The J Curve*, "For a country that is 'stable because it's closed' to become a country that is 'stable because it is open,' it must go through a transitional period of dangerous instability."[45] These are thoughtful security considerations that must be weighted by policymakers. Unfortunately, Cuba's present politico-economic system cannot be the starting point for a serious development and reconstruction process. The country's existing bureaucratic, institutional, and organizational framework is not conducive to the creation of a new state.

It is precisely to contain instability, if it can be contained at all, that the hard choices must be left in the hands of the Cuban people in a process of democratic participation. The social dislocations brought about by decollectivization and desocialization policies must be supported by a citizenry that has confidence in the legitimacy of a system of independent institutions. Democracy allows for the legitimate and constructive expression of discontent. By definition, citizen participation is non-existant when politico-economic decisions are made without transparency by a cabal of mandarins. In other words, if instability is to be minimized, democratic freedoms and citizenry participation are

---

45   Bremmer, Ian. *The J Curve*. New York. Simon & Schuster. 2006.

essential. If, as Brenner suggests, instability is inevitable, then the idea of waiving democracy for the sake of stability is a false choice. Putting off democratic reforms from immediate consideration only postpones the inevitable. If instability is the concern, a democratic platform for reforms offers a much more positive and acceptable outlet for social frustrations than an authoritarian platform.

In this context we can revisit the experiences of China, Vietnam, Estonia, and the Czech Republic. In the cases of China and Vietnam, we can expect in the years to come either serious political instability or a continuation of totalitarianism. In contrast, Estonia and the Czech Republic are now not only prosperous but also open and stable. Instability was minimized not by withholding freedom but by engaging the citizenry from the very beginning in the process of change.

Chapter III – Search for Meaning

We have come to know Man as he really is.
After all, man is that being who invented the
gas chambers at Auschwitz; however, he is
also that being who entered those gas
chambers upright, with the Lord's prayer or
the *Shema Yisrael* on his lips.

Viktor E. Frankl

To this point, the discussion has emphasized two main themes: the dire situation with respect to Cuba's civil society and values, and the absolute necessity for individual freedoms and empowerment contemporaneous with and as part of any legitimate transition process. In short, the civic knowledge, skills, and virtues most needed for a successful *mañana* in Cuba are precisely what are most lacking and what will be the most difficult to reconstruct. These conditions paint Cuba's future into the proverbial corner. The psychological way out, poetically expressed, is simple: "If it is a despot you would dethrone, see first that his throne erected within you is destroyed."[46] The practical way out of this dilemma is much more daunting.

There are many ways to define civil society in the modern sense. Civil society is, at its core, a political concept where the focal point is on the role of the individual citizens in social, political, and economic

---

46   Gibran, Kahlil. *The Prophet*. New York. Alfred A Knopf. 1991: 53

activities and institutions. Its key function is to limit the power of the state and, as such, it is essential for effective democratic governance. It cannot flourish in a culture of fear, which destroys the trust necessary for a thriving civil society. A civil society can only hope to dethrone the despot within each citizen if it is free from fear. But a psychological culture of fear can persist in a society in transition even after a repressive government has been replaced in a formal sense. It is a very grave intellectual and practical misstep to deem that Castroism ends with the disappearance of the Castro brothers. A new democratic regime may remove the fear of political persecution, for example, but it may imbue society with a new set of fears. Democracies and market economies can be messy, particularly to those unaccustomed to their vicissitudes. Market economies are by definition disorganized and seemingly chaotic, except as governed by Adam Smith's invisible hand.

In this context, it is helpful to reflect on some conditions and their opposites that are typically present in a society as it transitions from authoritarianism to democracy.[47] Whereas authoritarian control is characterized by certainty, democratic governance ushers in uncertainty. Democratic governance replaces uniformity with diversity, and conformity gives way to individuality. Control and rigidity are supplanted by autonomy and flexibility. A society accustomed to stability and predictability must now face instability and unpredictability. Familiar dogmas are confused by pluralism, and centralization disintegrates into decentralization. It is no wonder that transitions encounter opposition and at times even a certain nostalgia for the old totalitarian systems.

Sustaining democracy is hard work, and the necessary freedom from fear requires more than formal legal protections. It requires, among other things, a psychological reconstruction of society at large. The most commonsensical, obvious, and often offered prescription is educational programs. Professor Andy Gomez, whose research agenda focuses on the ideological and psychological reconstruction of human values and attitudes in a post-Castro Cuba, argues that "the role of education in the future of Cuba will be one of the leading factors in

---

47   Gomez, Andy S. "The Role of Education in Cuba's Future." *ICCAS*. 2008: 7

transforming the psychological values and attitudes of the population in order to develop a civil society and eventually sustain a democratic state."[48]

Clearly, as we have learned in nation-building efforts throughout the world, it is easier to build a new parliament building than it is to populate that building with legislators committed to democratic values and governance. But the efficacy of formal education programs to convey civic values is highly questionable beyond primary school. Even the most comprehensive indoctrination programs used by the Cuban regime over decades have proven to be less than effective in creating the communist "new man" that was to be communal in outlook and sacrificial in his labor for the common good. Perhaps this failure can be blamed on a "new man" concept inherently antithetical to human nature. The point is made only to highlight the limitations of formal civic education programs so that we do not dilate its possibilities.

A program of civic education is a necessary but insufficient remedy. Civic knowledge curricula, as Gomez argues, must include key concepts alien to most of the Cuban population, such as the rule of law, limited government, representative government, individual rights, popular sovereignty, and voluntary political participation. On the other hand, the development of civic skills and civic virtues require much more than classroom learning. Civil skills require the practical application of civic knowledge to civic life. Civic knowledge taught in an experiential vacuum without the opportunity of actual practice becomes theoretical knowledge rather than an empirical approach to governing. The same "put into practice" requirement holds true for civic virtues such as self-discipline, civility, compassion, and tolerance. Of these three components of democratic civic education, civic knowledge is most amenable to classroom curricula. Civil skills and civil values are primarily experiential in nature. There is no question that a program of civil education emphasizing democratic citizenship is necessary to develop a civil society capable of sustaining a democratic society, but it should be viewed as only one necessary component of a more comprehensive effort. Civil education is an arduous, long-term process

---

48 Gomez, Andy S. "The Role of Education in Cuba's Future." p 2.

that will take generations to impact Cuba's political culture. Moreover, civil education, without the opportunity for civic participation is doomed to failure.

The Despot Within – Democracy ¡Para Que? (What For?)

The legacy of Castroism is an imposing range of obstacles for any democratic transition. It is not just a "simple" matter of economic or ideological reconstruction. A successful transition in Cuba requires a psychological reconstruction. This task is particularly difficult in an environment of uncertainty, diversity, individuality, autonomy, flexibility, instability, unpredictability, pluralism, and decentralization; that is to say, in an environment of democratic governance. And yet, that is how it must be. The very first step, however, is recognition of the despot within—of the values that subvert democratic governance. "The seed of the despot is in every man."[49]

Cuban folklore—at least in the exile community—has begun to acknowledge with characteristic informality and humor this despot within. In her song *"Nosotros los Cubanos"* ("We Cubans"), composer/interpreter Marisela Verena caricaturizes with witty and explicit lyrics the essence of the Cuban character. She sings, "The world is divided exactly in half, we Cubans and the rest of humanity. We are not political ... We Cubans do not go to hell. We pay on Earth with awful governments. We are never wrong. It is never our fault. The other guy is responsible because he is a *comemierda*."

It loses in the translation, of course, but the song makes a profound statement of Cuban ethnocentrism and of the "despot within" trait. Her song concludes that "all would surely be happier if the world would follow our commands."

---

49 All the English translations of José Marti's thoughts cited, at times without direct attribution, are from Ripoll, Carlos, ed. *Marti, Thoughts/Pensamientos A Bilingual Anthology.* New York. Eliseo Torres & Sons. 1985

Cuban intellectual Luis Aguilar León's classic parody article *"He Aquí Que el Profeta Habla de los Cubanos"* (It Is Here That the Prophet Speaks of Cubans) is a most eloquent example of this introspection:[50]

> Cubans are among you, but they are not of you. Do not attempt to know them, because their souls live in the impenetrable world of dualism ...

> Do not ever argue with them. Cubans are born with immanent wisdom. They do not need to read; they know it all. They do not need to travel; they have seen it all. Cubans have elected themselves as the chosen people.

> ... To bring together Cubans is easy; to unite them, impossible. A Cuban is capable of anything in this world except to win the applause of other Cubans. When they argue, they do not say, "I do not agree with you." They say, "You are completely and totally wrong."

It is interesting to point out that these insights of the despot within are not universally prevalent even within the Cuban exile community. Even in a community that has experienced decades of living and learning in freedom outside Cuba, and has had the opportunity to live out the application of civic knowledge to civic life, these introspections tend to originate with artists and intellectuals. This observation coincides with the results (introduced in Chapter I) of the interviews conducted by Freedom House in Cuba where only artists and intellectuals were concerned with the lack of civil and political rights. It appears that the efficacy of democratic civic education (for Cubans at least) is limited, even in fully democratic settings where civic knowledge can be applied and practiced as civil skills and civic values. The evidence is perhaps anecdotal, but the divisions, intransigence, and incivility of debate prevalent in the exile community attest to this "cultural tendency

---

50 These excerpts are my translation. The original Spanish full text can be found in: Aguilar León, Luis. *Cuba y su Futuro*. Miami. Ediciones Universal. 1992: 186.

of Cubans to construe politics as a moral crusade for absolute ends" —what Damian Fernandez calls the politics of passion.[51] The crucial distinction between a political adversary or opponent and an enemy is rarely considered in Cuban discourse.

It is within this unfortunate framework of the proclivities in Cuban political culture for messianic absolutism that the "economic reforms first and political reforms will follow" thesis must be examined and rejected. It is a path precariously similar to Fidel Castro's *"Revolución primero, elecciones después"* (Revolution first, elections later). In 1959, when Castro betrayed his pledge to hold elections and reestablish constitutional liberties, he introduced the "Revolution first, elections later" slogan to rationalize his actions. In short order, his official propaganda machinery abandoned the "elections later" portion of the slogan and replaced it with *"Elecciones, ¿para que?"* (Elections, what for?)

If Cuba's path is one of "economic reforms first and political reforms later," it is a fair bet that the collective political paralysis and passivity prevalent in Cuba's political culture, together with the absence of democratic institutions, and the ever-present "despot within" trait will result in a repeat performance of the 1959 abandonment of democratic reforms. Political reforms, what for?

"What's Past Is Prologue"[52]

If Shakespeare was right, and the past is prologue, it is essential for Cubans to apprehend the reality that the death of a tyrant does not equal the death of tyranny. It particularly does not mean that the despot within is vanquished. For democracy to succeed, Cubans must abandon the mythologies of the "maximum leader" and achieve a sort of sociopolitical mental health. If they do not, the past will be prologue to despotic continuity masquerading as change.   .

---

51   Fernandez, Damian J. pp 7.

52   Shakespeare, William. *The Tempest*, act II, scene I, lines 253-54.

Cuba's "body politic" is unwell. Aguilar León writes about how in 1959 Cuba became a *"kranken volk,"* a sick nation that applauded its own crushing.[53] Without overstating the applicability of organic analogies to politics, it is evident that Cubans today suffer from a broken spirit, a collective national melancholy. It is a paralyzing sadness without vestige of trust. In the early days, Cubans jocularly labeled the revolution *"La revolución del callo pisado."* The implication was that Cubans only complained when they were personally impacted by Castro's edicts. Eventually, of course, all Cubans were affected, but until they were, many believed they themselves would be reprieved. Democratic citizenship requires precisely the opposite attitude; that is, a heartfelt preoccupation with the civil liberties and political rights of everyone. In other words, Cubans need to leave behind their preference for the "politics of anti-politics."[54]

The dangers of political apathy are poignantly captured in the popular poem "First they came ..."[55] about the inactivity of German intellectuals following the Nazi rise to power and the sequential purging of various groups:

> First they came for the communists, and I did not speak out—because I was not a communist;
>
> Then they came for the socialists, and I did not speak out—because I was not a socialist;
>
> Then they came for the trade unionists, and I did not speak out—because I was not a trade unionist;
>
> Then they came for the Jews, and I did not speak out—because I was not a Jew;
>
> Then they came for me—and there was no one left to speak for me.

---

53 Aguilar León, Luis. *Cuba y su Futuro.* p.76

54 Gutiérrez-Boronat, Orlando. *Cuba: A Nation in Search of a State.* 2008. Gutiérrez-Boronat argues that "The politics of anti-politics led to Castroism"

55 The poem is attributed to Pastor Martin Niemöller (1892–1984)

It is one thing to identify and pontificate about what ails Cuban society and quite another to figure out the remedy. An unlikely source of inspiration may be found in the experiences and work of an Auschwitz survivor who found meaning in the words of Nietzsche: "He who has a Why to live for can bear almost any How."

In 1959, coincidental with the onset of Cuba's paralyzing sadness, Viktor Frankl first published *Man's Search for Meaning*, his riveting descriptions of life in Nazi death camps and its lessons for spiritual survival.[56] For three years, Frankl, a psychiatrist, labored in Nazi concentration camps, including Auschwitz, while his parents, brother, and pregnant wife perished. While the analogy is far from perfect, life in Castro's Cuba can be analyzed from the standpoint of how life in a concentration camp—life without freedoms—is reflected in the mind of the average person. The study of the unrelenting struggle for daily sustenance and for life itself contributes to our understanding of the psychopathology of peoples under stress. For example, the "*revolución del callo pisado*" phenomenon described above parallels a psychiatric condition known as "delusion of reprieve" where "the condemned man, immediately before his execution, gets the illusion that he might be reprieved at the very last minute."[57] In the early stages of the Cuban revolution, the various segments of Cuban society sequentially suffered from this delusion of reprieve as other segments and industrial sectors were successively stricken.

In his work, Frankl describes how after an initial phase of denial and delusions, the prisoners entered a phase of relative apathy and emotional death, blunting emotions and feelings. This dimming of reality was a necessary mechanism of self-defense to center all emotions and efforts on daily existence. The constant necessity of concentrating on the task of staying alive—in Cuba's case, concentrating on bread-and-butter issues—resulted in a "regression" or retreat to a more primitive form of mental life. "The camp inmate was frightened of making decisions and of taking any sort of initiative whatsoever. This

---

56   Frankl, Viktor E. *Man's Search for Meaning*. Boston. Beakon Press. 2006.

57   Ibid., p. 10

was the result of a strong feeling that fate was one's own master."[58] In his psychological presentation and psychopathological explanations of the characteristics of a concentration camp inmate, Frankl asks about human liberty. "Is there no spiritual freedom in regard to behavior and reaction to any given surroundings?" Is man no more than a product of conditional and environmental factors? Can man escape the influences of his surroundings? He concludes that the experiences of concentration camp life show that man does have a choice of action, that apathy can be overcome, and man can preserve his spiritual freedom. In his view, it is precisely this spiritual freedom—which cannot be taken away—that makes life meaningful and purposeful.

Frankl's observations of his fellow prisoners convinced him that those who lost their inner hold on their moral and spiritual selves eventually fell victim to the camp's degenerating influences. The most perverting influence on one's moral and spiritual self was not knowing how long the term of imprisonment would be. Psychologists refer to this condition as a "provisional existence of unknown limit." In a provisional existence state, everything tends to become pointless. Cubans have for over five decades experienced a provisional existence of unknown limit. Cubans, like the men in the concentration camps who cannot see the end of their provisional existence, are not able to aim for life's ultimate goals. They experience an existence without a future and without a goal.

Following Frankl's work, to conquer the psychopathological influence of the life without freedoms that Cubans have endured for so long, it is necessary for Cubans to regain faith in a future they can look forward to. "The prisoner who had lost faith in the future—his future—was doomed. With his loss of belief in the future, he also lost his spiritual hold; he let himself decline and became subject to mental and physical decay."[59] While life in concentration camps cannot be compared in absolute terms with the lack of freedoms in Cuba, the psychopathological profiles offer insights. In both cases, a fundamental change in attitude toward life plays a pivotal role. For current *Mañana*

---

58 Ibid., p. 56

59 Ibid., p. 74

in Cuba purposes, the third stage in Frankl's taxonomy is particularly useful: the psychology of the prisoner after liberation. In his words, "Life in a concentration camp tore open the human soul and exposed its depth," so that the released prisoner could not fully escape the influences of the brutality which had surrounded him. In similar fashion, the psychological influence of Castroism will endure in Cuban civil society. The way out of this existential distress is not just freedom from deplorable physical conditions, e.g., economic reforms; it is the personal freedom to take a stand on conditions. Cuba's potentialities will be contingent not just on conditions, but on decisions. More to the point, Cuba's potentialities will depend more on individual freedoms and empowerment than on a given set of economic reforms.

One reason for this psychological exploration is to emphasize, from a different intellectual angle, the inadequacy of economic reforms without hand-in-hand individual freedoms and empowerment. A successful transition in Cuba requires, perhaps above all else, a compelling vision of hope for all Cubans; an undeniable revelation that life can regain its potential meaning despite its tragic aspects. It requires a visualization of the future that does not equate the dignity of a society with its economic gains.

Chapter IV – The First Law

Where there is enlightened liberty not even
age-old angers can sink their teeth and raise
storms. Rather, they melt and crumble, like
a comet in its collision with the sun.

José Marti

"I WANT THE FIRST LAW of our republic to be the reverence of Cubans for the full dignity of man ..."[60]

A pernicious legacy of Castroism is its appropriation and rewriting of Cuban history to serve its own purposes and ideology. For five decades, Cubans have been taught a manipulated revisionism of their country's history and particularly of the political thoughts of Cuba's foremost patriot, José Marti. Since Marti's death in combat in 1895, his inspirational words have been used, overused, and often distorted or taken out of context by every Cuban political figure. It is therefore with some reluctance and misgivings that this chapter calls generously on José Marti. On the other hand, a successful transition in Cuba needs to resurrect the best of the country's historic legacy, much of which comes to life in Marti. His ethical foundation and passion for democratic principles can serve to guide a thorny discussion in this chapter. Not Marti the dreamer, the idealist, the poet; his teachings, not

---

60 All the English translations of José Marti's thoughts cited here, at times without direct attribution, are from Ripoll, Carlos, ed. *Marti, Thoughts/Pensamientos A Bilingual Anthology*. New York. Eliseo Torres & Sons. 1985

as misused in political demagoguery, but Marti in the most practical applicability of his words. The discussion here accesses Marti as a gifted social scientist with a profound understanding of freedom as the only workable environment for the pursuit of a happy human existence.

Considerations for a successful Cuban transition begin with a thoughtful appreciation that the Cuban Diaspora has in fact created two distinct Cuban communities, one on the island and one in exile. Each of these communities, in turn, can be subdivided by any number of demographic and psychographic factors. The net effect is that of various dissimilar communities with divergent sociopolitical and economic views. In a political sense, these communities are analogous to discrete constituencies, each with its own agenda and vision of the Cuban state. Recalling the pronouncement of Aguilar Leon's prophet that " ...to bring together Cubans is easy, to unite them impossible," this ideological diversity presents a monumental challenge. Paradoxically, this diversity also embodies the best opportunity to build, in the Cuba of tomorrow, a modern politico-economic system unimpeded by the obsolete institutional structures of a communist state. Let's approach the topic by bringing up first the exile community.

Four distinctive waves of Cuban migration to the United States can be identified. The first (1959–62) consisted primarily of upper to upper-middle class families. The second wave (1965–74) represented mostly middle and working class families. The Mariel boatlift wave of the 1980s was predominantly lower income. The same is more or less the case with the *balseros* (rafters) wave that began with Cuba's Special Period in the early 1990s.[61] Not only are the demographic profiles of these four emigration waves dissimilar, but there are marked psychographic, ethical, and cultural differences. Just as importantly, there are dramatic differences with respect to the conceptions of the role of the state and the individual in society. During the Mariel boatlift, Cubans from the first two waves were surprised, perhaps even scandalized, by the attitudes, mores, and even physical appearance of their newly arrived compatriots. Some would comment pejoratively,

---

61   Cuba's Special Period in Peacetime refers to the severe economic crises the country experienced after the collapse of the Soviet Union in 1991.

"No parecen cubanos." ("They do not look like Cubans.") In fact, it can be said that each wave of exiles came from a different sociopolitical and economic Cuba. As such, each wave embodies its own perceptions of the conditions that caused their exodus.

Much more can be said, often controversially, about these distinct waves of Cuban migration. Sociologists point out that the Cuban Diaspora holds both various waves (defined by timing) and various "vintages" (defined by attitudes) and have sought to describe their social characteristics with colorful labels: "those who wait," "those who escape," "those who search," "those who hope," and "those who despair."[62] What is evident, however, is that the various waves possessed different sets of social resources and varied in social class, race, education, family, institutional knowledge, and values. Clearly, here we are engaging in gross generalizations and oversimplifications with a redeeming expository goal. For purposes of this discussion, it will be controversial enough to dichotomize the Cuban Diaspora into two groups: Political exiles "pushed out" by political variables, and economic immigrants "pulled out" by the prospects of better economic opportunities. In the most universal fashion, the first two waves of "pushed out" Cuban emigrants share the characteristics and views of political exiles, and the later arrivals appear to think and act more as "pulled out" economic immigrants.

Both economic immigrants and political exiles dream of a romanticized return or visit to their homeland. This is typically the case, not just for Cubans, but for all refugees. Those that emigrated primarily for economic reasons, however, aspire to return to their birthplace when their personal economic situation allows it, perhaps in their golden years. Political exiles, on the other hand, are not prepared to return until the oppressive conditions that prompted their exodus are no longer present. From the exile's point of view, returning is not an option ruled by personal conditions or motives, but one centered on the conditions affecting his countrymen. The act of going into exile is a political statement against collective injustice. By definition, the political exile that surrenders to his personal melancholy by returning

---

62   Pedraza, Silvia. "Cuba's Refugees: Manifold Migrations." *ASCE.* 1995

without a fundamental change in the conditions that brought about his exit relinquishes his label of political exile and becomes an immigrant. Marti, in this instance speaking as a fighter for independence, was harsh in his judgment, "To visit the oppressor's house is to sanction oppression."

But the Cuban reality is that after five decades of valiantly opposing oppression, many nostalgic exiles have elected to visit their homeland. Some are motivated by understandable humanitarian reasons; to share once again, perhaps for the last time, in the company of a loved one, or to bring comfort to one in need. Thus two main forces have come into play in the Cuban Diaspora: the different demographic and psychographic profiles of the emigration waves, and the sheer mental exhaustion of prolonged exile. The end result is that, by definition, the Cuban-American community has shifted, in some measure, from a community of political exiles to one of immigrants. This, in turn, has for the most part settled the community into essentially the two political camps with different approaches to Cuba's future that were introduced in the first paragraph of this work. One constituency places individual freedoms and empowerment front and center and the other advocates the primacy of economic measures even if undertaken outside the framework of democratic empowerment.

This division in the Cuban-American community does not imply that civil liberties and political rights have lost their significance or that they are any less critical for a successful transition. Notwithstanding the motivations to emigrate that may serve to define the Cuban exodus as economic or political, all societies are both political and economic. Freedoms in the political and economic realms are not easily disentangled. Marti the philosopher notes, "Man loves liberty, even if he does not know that he loves it. He is driven by it and flees from where it does not exist."

"Every Man Is Obliged to Overcome His Bitterness."

Healing this wound within the Cuban-American community may be challenging, but it is only a microcosm of the much deeper, varied, and widespread wounds that must be healed in Cuba itself to bring about a successful transition. "The war against hate," Marti noted, "is perhaps the last essential, definitive, and legitimate war." This essential war against hate can only be carried out in an institutional milieu of enlightened liberty. In other words, healing the Cuban nation requires a tolerant political process. Marti the politician explains, "Politics is the art of raising unjust humanity towards justice, of reconciling the selfish beast with the generous angel, of favoring and harmonizing various interests, with virtue and the general welfare as its goals." The healing of the Cuban nation cannot take place in a political vacuum, it cannot take place in a totalitarian setting, and it cannot take place without the civil liberties and political rights to practice heroic tolerance and political wisdom.

The political challenges and disputes faced by the Cuban communities outside the island are miniscule when compared with the political and social challenges that will be encountered when Cuba undertakes a genuine transition. How communism was imposed in Cuba is well-known history. How it ends will influence the transition process and the quantitative and qualitative implementation of changes in personnel, political processes, economic programs, and institutional reforms. In all likelihood, the end of communism in Cuba will come about in a way unique to Cuba. Nonetheless, important generic lessons can be learned from the transition experience of the East European countries. Fredo Arias King, an expert on post-Soviet democratization with encyclopedic knowledge of the East European transition experiences, classifies the countries end-game experiences into eight groups:[63]

---

63 Arias King, Fredo. *Transiciones: La Experiencia de Europa Del Este*. Buenos Aires. Fund. Cadal, Fudacion Pontis, and CEON. 2005. I have taken some liberties in translating this taxonomy from Fredo Arias King's original Spanish work. The interested reader is referred to this excellent study.

Overthrow—The first group is one where communism ended when dissidents were able to overthrow an obstinate communist party and form a new government made up primarily of dissidents. Fredo Arias King places Czechoslovakia, East Germany, Yugoslavia, Kyrgyzstan, and Georgia in this group.

Substitution—In the second group, the communist parties were more flexible and were willing to negotiate a transition. This was the case in Poland, Lithuania, Estonia, and Slovenia.

Transformation—In group three, the principal communist leaders took the initiative toward regime change without the presence of great social pressures. Examples are the Soviet Union (1985), Hungary (1956), and Czechoslovakia (1968).

Reappearance—Group four is represented by countries in which former high-level government officials who had been removed from power used the nascent democratic movement to return to power. Russia, Romania, and Croatia make up this group.

Replacement—The fifth group is characterized by groups of mid-level government officials from the regime's nomenclature who took advantage of the moment to take up the flag of democratic or nationalistic reform to undermine the regime they served. Such was the case in Hungary (1989), Serbia (1989), and Bulgaria.

Reincarnation—The sixth group of countries is one were the state parties felt great social pressure to fake a brake with communism in order to survive, although they were not always successful in their effort. Examples are Ukraine, Moldova, Albania, Mongolia, Macedonia, and Latvia.

Continuity—In the seventh group, the fall of communism arrived only in appearances. The existing communist leaders unexpectedly turned into the leaders of independent nations, but retained the principal structures of repression and the command economy. This was the situation in Uzbekistan, Kazakhstan, Turkmenistan, and Belarus.

Violence—The eighth group in Arias King's taxonomy is made up of leaders who used state violence to provoke civil wars and thus retain and aggrandize their power. Tajikistan, Serbia, Armenia, and Azerbaijan make up this group.

Fredo Arias King's classifications are *ex-post-facto* based on his study of the historical East European experience. They can, however, be used prospectively as potential generic scenarios for how a transition may proceed in Cuba. Before doing so, it is important, in an abundance of analytical caution, to point out the obvious: Cuba is not Eastern Europe. Cuba's transition experience will be distinctly Cuban. Its history is not that of a country occupied by Soviet forces. The pivotal role played in some East European countries by institutions such as the Communist Party, the Catholic Church, or the labor movement will differ. The extent of government control of the economy, and the post-communism economic starting points are also different. The same holds true for the strength and unity of dissident movements and many other factors. In addition, two other differentiating factors are required for this discussion. First is the overt or covert influence of Castroism, a legacy that, as was argued above, will not disappear with the disappearance of its namesakes. And second is the presence of a large constituency of immigrants (as redefined here) and exiles.

"To Change Masters Is Not to Be Free"

Given the heroic, but fragmented state of the Cuban dissidence on the island, it is highly unlikely that Cuban communism will come to an end via a dissident-led **overthrow**. The same holds true of the Catholic Church, and the government-controlled labor organizations. Similarly, Cuba's Communist Party has never been a determinant player in Cuba's politics, as some of the Communist Parties were in Eastern Europe; thus the **substitution** scenario is also unlikely. **Transformation** from the top, **reappearance,** or **replacement** are also improbable, given the apparent leadership succession profile of hard-line loyalists such as Machado Ventura, Ramiro Valdés Menéndez, Ulises Rosales del Toro, and others. **Violence** in the sense of a prolonged civil war or armed struggle for power is doubtful, except perhaps internally within the Cuban Armed Forces (FAR). This analysis leaves essentially two prospective scenarios, both led by the Cuban Armed Forces, the dominant player in Cuba's polity: **reincarnation** and **continuity**.

In the Cuban case, Arias King's eight scenarios can de distilled into two, both suggesting the undesirable result of continuity disguised as change. This is the Gordian knot of the transitional challenges for Cuba, since neither outcome removes the institutional impediments to democracy by providing transparency and accountability. Neither outcome places individual freedoms and empowerment front and center. Both reinforce Cuba's militaristic caste system. "All unchecked power exercised over a long time degenerates into a caste system. With castes come vested interests, high positions, fear of losing them, intrigues to sustain them."

Overlaying this appraisal is the large constituency of immigrants and exiles, a constituency once made up primarily of political exiles, but shifting, with the unforgiving passage of time, into one of immigrants. The use of the term "constituency" here, instead of the most commonly used term "community," is deliberate to highlight a point. It is a constituency that can influence and be influenced by U.S.-Cuba policy. Most importantly for this discussion, however, it is a constituency that can be influenced by the Cuban government for its own survival purposes. Recalling that we are defining immigrants as a constituency that aspires to return to their birthplace when their personal economic situation allows it, it is a constituency that can be readily co-opted by minimalist reforms in Cuba. It is a constituency that can be persuaded by economic measures even if undertaken outside the framework of democratic empowerment. This is particularly the case with occasional tourist-like travel by immigrants who are not seeking a permanent return. This is not a judgmental statement, simply an effort to depict a reality. The Cuban government can seek to improve economic conditions by acting to satisfy the non-political desires of Cuban immigrants that do not threaten the regime.

The second part of this reality is the dwindling exile constituency as a reservoir of democratic orientation for Cuba. That is, the generational dwindling of a constituency of historic political exiles.

Award-winning Cuban blogger Yoani Sanchez, describing with her poetic flair the increasing disillusionment in Cuba, writes:

> Mathematics confronts us with certain infallible truths: the number of those dissatisfied grows, but the group of those who applaud gains no new "souls."
>
> As in an hourglass, every day hundreds of the small particles of the disillusioned come to a stop just opposite the place where they once were ...
> The time to multiply and add passed ... now the abacuses operate always by subtracting, marking the interminable flight in a single direction.[64]

A comparable inexorable hourglass affliction is at play in the historical exile constituency. In the short-term, the likely **reincarnation** or **continuity** scenarios for *mañana* in Cuba will entice the visits of the immigrant constituency but will not usher a genuine transition. The increasing unidirectional disillusionment that Yoani Sanchez describes will not turn into a political force, but rather into a continuing exodus, or into "those who concentrate on the peaceful work of caring for their grandchildren and waiting in line for bread."[65] By this time, there will not be a hand left able to turn the hourglass of Cuba's totalitarianism. For Cubans to break out of this Gordian knot, "it is necessary to make virtue fashionable" —democratic virtue.

---

64 Sanchez, Yoani. "Reloj de Arena." *Generación Y.* February, 2009. http://www. desdecuba.com/generaciony/?p=706

65 Ibid.

Chapter V – No Le Pidas Peras Al Olmo (Do Not Ask Pears of the Elm)

If liberty and equality, as is thought by
some, are chiefly to be found in democracy,
they will be best attained when all persons
alike share in the government to the utmost.

Aristotle

CUBANS ON THE ISLAND HAVE either never experienced liberty or have forgotten how to feel free. Their concept of democracy has been perverted by decades of Marxist-Leninist indoctrination, rhetorical distortions, and their government's exhortation of Cuba as the most perfect form of democracy. They do not know, and cannot be expected to know, what a modern democratic society looks like, how it functions, or how one goes about building it. Cubans outside the island, like many other free peoples, take it for granted as they go on in freedom with their daily lives. More often than not, democracy is viewed and popularly defined simply as a constitutional form of government; a specific methodology by which free peoples elect their leaders. Democracy is much more.

Unfortunately, hand-in-hand with the shifting profile of the Cuban-American community—51 percent of whom arrived in the U.S. after 1991—the very "reason for being" of the Cuban polemic has shifted for a sizable segment of the community. What is, and should be, fundamentally a decorous struggle for freedoms has metamorphosed into a street fight to influence U.S. foreign policy. Cubans have taken their eyes off the ball—and, to abuse the metaphor, are striking out. The uplifting cry for freedom has lost its virtue and has been replaced by the uninspiring cry for a change in U.S. foreign policy. This shift of focus is disquieting because, notwithstanding all their idiosyncratic imperfections, the Cuban Diaspora—both political exiles and economic immigrants—remains the Cuban nation's most resourceful reservoir of democratic values. They are the only ones who have had an opportunity to experience institutional environments committed to the defense and preservation of civil liberties and political rights. As such, the Cuban-American community is uniquely positioned to offer civic and democratic orientation to their countrymen on the island.

The maxim *"No le pidas peras al olmo"* ("Do not ask pears of the elm") suggests that we cannot expect what is not possible.[66] That is to say, a successful transition in Cuba must take place within the realm of the possible. This in turn requires a justice-bound, but non-exclusionary, non-elitist approach to policymaking designed for the rebuilding of the nation; a sort of cultural sociopolitical syncretism that redefines the very reason for being of the Cuba of tomorrow. Sociopolitical syncretism in this usage is the attempt to reconcile disparate or contrary beliefs, not by melding practices of various schools of thought, but by offering a supra-ideological unifying point. For transitional leaders and policymakers, even the most compelling political or economic arguments cannot be expected to result in a national sociopolitical policymaking consensus. Even if such a state of affairs were possible, it would only set the stage for disillusionments when the anticipated (or promised) results failed to materialize in short order. The various Cuban constituencies must find their sociopolitical syncretism in a domain that transcends political and economic ideologies; that supra-politico-economic domain is freedom.

In our day-to-day usage, the terms liberty, freedom, and even democracy tend to be used interchangeably as synonyms. Here we need to be somewhat more precise and descriptive. The proposition that the

---

66   A Spanish version of "You can't get blood from a turnip."

concept of freedom rather than any particular "ism" (e.g., socialism, capitalism) offers a more unifying platform for post-Castro Cuba flows from sociopolitical pragmatism rather than idealism. Given the vast differences in sociopolitical and economic values and ideologies that exist in the Cuban nation—inside and outside the island—it is unrealistic to think that the traditional philosophical platforms of individualism, collectivism, etc., can serve as unifying platforms. In addition, the discussion in Chapter IV suggests that the most likely transition scenarios of **reincarnation** or **continuity** offer little opportunity for a genuine paradigm shift. Among other reasons, the dependency on the state as the principal provider of goods and services that has developed over fifty years will pervade Cuban society for at least a generation after the demise of Castroism. Post-Castro Cuban leaders will find no consensus regarding the legitimate role of the state in the rebuilding of the nation. These debates, regarding the role of the state in society, permeate Latin American politics today, even after they have subsided or taken on a different political form in other regions of the world.

Whereas socialism, capitalism, and all the other "isms" are divisive *per se*, freedom is a much more universally accepted rallying point for reforms. It is a functional way to address Aguilar Leon's dictum that " …to bring Cubans together is easy, to unite them impossible." Freedom, as the focal point, is a no-nonsense way to address strategic and political differences. The Cuban struggle, now and in the future, needs to be re-postulated as an ongoing struggle for freedoms. It is perhaps the only philosophical concept capable of bridging the vast differences in sociopolitical and economic values and ideologies that exist in the Cuban nation. Interestingly, however, the word freedom in English has no literal translation in Spanish (other than liberty) in the sense that we distinguish freedom from liberty in intellectual discourse. This linguistic and etymological peculiarity imposes the philosophical sidetrack that follows.

Freedom and Liberty

Freedom, or the idea of being free, is a far-reaching concept with abundant interpretations by philosophers and schools of thought. For current purposes, it is only necessary to note, and to immediately set aside, the philosophical concept of freedom that concerns itself with the metaphysical questions of free will versus determinism. Broadly speaking, the discussion here focuses on political freedom, which is, in and of itself, a broad concept.

Aung San Suu Kyi's exhortation offered in Chapter II to "Feel always free" and the concomitant observation that Cubans on the island have forgotten how to feel free offer a logical starting point for this discussion. Aung San Suu Kyi's maxim, perhaps due to her Buddhist and sociopolitical beliefs, embodies metaphysical as well as the positive and negative connotations of freedom. Latvian-British philosopher and historian of ideas Isaiah Berlin postulated the important distinction between "freedom from" (negative freedom) and "freedom to" (positive freedom). Negative freedom refers to freedom from oppression, while positive freedom refers to freedom to develop one's potential. Freedom from designates a negative condition where an individual is protected from tyranny and the arbitrary exercise of authority, and freedom to designates not restraint, but having the means or opportunity to act.

In political philosophy, the interaction of the various ideas of positive and negative freedoms gives rise to the tensions and conflicts that the concept of freedom contains. For some, a person may be free from constraints and threats that nonetheless may leave that person free to do little in an environment without resources to exercise that freedom. When the notion of freedom is overextended in the positive sense, it leads some to an enabling interpretation that includes freedom from poverty, treatable disease, and more. Thus in the welfare socialist view, being free in the extreme positive sense of being enabled to requires whatever constraints are necessary by the state to freedom from in order to achieve a satisfactory distribution of society's output. This, of course, infringes on freedom from.

The more limited concept of political freedom is related to the concepts of civil liberties and individual rights. Typically, these include freedom of assembly, association, movement; freedom of the press, religion, speech, thought, and the like. In most democratic societies, these are afforded the legal protection of the state. A closely related concept in political philosophy is that of individualism. The individualist theory of government holds that the state should protect the freedoms of individuals to act as they wish, as long as they do not infringe on the freedoms of others.

The philosophical plot thickens when we bring in the controversial concept of economic freedom, which, in the liberal tradition, emphasizes free markets and private property but can also be viewed from a welfare redistributive perspective. Socialists who argue against the liberal conception of freedom contend that freedom has to be balanced against other values in a way that it is legitimate for the state to encroach on freedoms. Others view socialist policies as a slippery slope that can lead to totalitarianism, since wealth cannot be redistributed without coercion or force being used against individuals, which in turn reduces individual freedoms. For current purposes, it is most useful to stay with the classical liberal view that defines economic freedom in terms of freedom to produce, trade, and consume goods and services. Economic freedom is enshrined in the rule of law, property rights, and freedom of contract. Economic freedom is characterized by internal and external commercial openness, the protection of property rights, and freedom to undertake economic initiatives or entrepreneurship.

In this context, Austrian-British economist and philosopher Friedrich Hayek argued that the certainty of the law has contributed more to the prosperity of the West than any other single factor. In his view, the generality and equality principles of the rule of law require that all legal rules apply equally to everyone. The requirement that the rule of law must apply not only to the governed but also to those holding political and coercive power can be seen as safeguards against the arbitrary restriction of freedoms. The principles of the generality and equality of the law work against special privileges or laws favoring some citizens at the expense of others. More controversially, Hayek argued that equality before the law is incompatible with government policies that seek to achieve material equality. In this argument, government's attempts at generating material equality restrict economic freedom and lead to unequal treatment of individuals and to a compulsory redistribution of income. Similarly, economist Milton Friedman sees property rights as a basic human right and an essential foundation for other human rights.

In our modern times, the concept of liberty is generally conceived as the concept of negative freedoms. A theory of liberty is therefore a theory of political freedoms. It is in this limited context that the Spanish word *"libertad"* is normally used in political discourse, as *libre de* (free from) oppression or coercion. Let's recall that the argument presented is that freedom needs to be the focal point where the various Cuban constituencies find their sociopolitical syncretism in a domain that transcends political and economic ideologies; that freedom is perhaps the only philosophical concept capable of bridging the vast differences in sociopolitical and economic values and ideologies that exist in the Cuban nation. *Libertad* therefore must be conceived and presented by post-Castro Cuban leaders in the broader meaning of freedom; not only as *libre de*, but also as *libre para* (free to).

The Western reader may consider this an unnecessary academic and pedantic discussion bordering on Wittgensteinian linguistics. But in the context of post-Castro Cuban political jockeying, it will turn out to be monumentally important. Not only is the term *libertad* limited in its day-to-day popular political interpretation, but the term has been perverted and distorted by the Castro regime. *Libertad* under Castroism has been identified with the dissident movement and equated with *libertinaje* or licentiousness, in the most pejorative connotations of the word as lacking legal or moral restraints, especially sexual restraints.

What will resonate politically in post-Castro Cuba is not just political rights, but also economic rights. Recall also the findings of the Cuban public opinion survey introduced in Chapter I, where the major concerns relate to bread-and-butter issues and only artists and intellectuals were concerned with the lack of civil and political liberties. Add to this the sizable component of the Cuban Diaspora that has not been "pushed out" by political variables, but "pulled out" by the prospects of better economic opportunities (Chapter IV).

A successful transition in Cuba will require a new set of values based on self-confidence, self-reliance, courage to fight for one's rights, entrepreneurship, greater social tolerance and social equality, respect for the rule of law, and aspiration for higher accomplishments. These values are not overtly or explicitly captured by *libertad* understood only as *libre de* in the Cuban and Latin American historical traditions. In the English language liberty, as the absence of coercion, depicts just a piece of the intellectual puzzle that is freedom. In Spanish, the term *libertad* must be pressed into service in the liberal tradition that finds freedom in the power of the individual to assert individual initiatives. For five decades of Castroism, Cubans did not experience freedom from oppression or freedom to pursue their individual dreams. In order to function as the antidote for the last five decades of totalitarian rule, *libertad* needs to stand for much more than the absence of coercion. It needs to free the imagination and skills of the Cuban nation. *Libertad* needs to stand for liberal democracy.

Democracy

The theory of democracy is an immensely complicated subject that exceeds the scope of this book. The discussions that follow will be necessarily imperfect and bounded. However, because Cubans have been taught for five decades that their form of government represents the most perfect form of democracy and that *libertad* equates with licentiousness, it is necessary to impose on the reader by extending this philosophical sidetrack.

It is relevant to clarify how the term democracy is used in this work and contrast it to how Castroism has perverted the concept of democracy. Otherwise, Cubans tomorrow would be perfectly justified in rejecting democratic governance. If what they have experienced for so long is democracy, they should want no part in it. Just as importantly, without a profound appreciation of democratic values, democracy in the Cuba of tomorrow could quickly flounder as the inevitable difficulties of rebuilding a country come into play. In the 1920s, democracy flourished, but the Great Depression brought disenchantment and many European, Latin American, and Asian countries turned to strong-man dictatorships. Cuba's historical experience, as outlined in Chapter I, points to its tendency to reverse course in favor of strong-man messianic dictatorships.

Even though democracy can be defined succinctly in terms of its Greek etymology as government of the people, there is no universally accepted theory of democracy. It will have to suffice here to simply note that democracy has been alternatively defined in terms of its many manifestations such as: representative, parliamentary, liberal, constitutional, direct, socialist, anarchist, and more. There are also numerous philosophical criticisms of democracy on grounds of voter irrationality and unpreparedness, mob rule, moral decay, political instability, short-termism, conflict of interests, slow governmental response, volatility, unsustainability, Western influence, and the like. For our purposes, it is enough to note the opposition to democracy on grounds of unsophisticated voters and the perennial argument that democracy's frequent policy changes are inimical to economic growth and unsuitable for developing countries that assign a high priority to economic development and the reduction of poverty.

Democracy is indeed imperfect, as Winston Churchill observed: "The best argument against democracy is a five-minute conversation with the average voter." But he also refuted his tongue-in-cheek assessment by noting that "Democracy is the worst form of government except for all those others that have been tried." If a working definition of democracy is required, Abraham Lincoln provided us a succinct and eloquent one in his Gettysburg address as a government "of the people, by the people, and for the people."

As offered and explained in this work, the term democracy is used as a shorthand expression for liberal democracy, a representative democracy in which the ability of the elected representatives to exercise decision-making power is subject to the rule of law. It is a democracy that is moderated by a constitution, that emphasizes the protection of the rights and freedoms of individuals, a democracy that places constraints on the leaders and on the extent to which the will of the majority can be exercised against the rights of the minorities.

As is the case with the term *libertad*, what will resonate politically and practically in post-Castro Cuba is not democracy as a noun, but liberal democracy as a governing ideal, a syllabus where leaders are constrained by the rule of law and where the protection of the rights and freedoms of individuals is emphasized. Somewhat paradoxically, it is this specific type of governing program that is best suited for the irreverent characteristics of the Cuban nation. It is this type of democracy that offers the best antidote, not only to the outer despots-in-the-making and tendencies of messianic absolutism, but just as importantly, it is the antidote for the despot within discussed in Chapter III.

Liberalism and Liberal Democracy

In general terms, liberalism entails a range of political philosophies that consider individual liberty and equality under the law to be the most important political goals. It emphasizes individual rights, equality of opportunities (not necessarily equal outcomes), and transparency in governance. Classical liberalism embraces the invisible hand of Adam Smith's *laissez-faire* economics as an organizing principle for society. Adam Smith postulated that the moral and economic life of individuals could be structured without state management.

Political liberalism holds that individuals, not the collective, are the basis of law and society. Economic liberalism argues that without individual property rights and freedom of contract, other liberties are impossible. In the twentieth century, liberalism defined itself as the antithesis of totalitarianism and collectivism. For liberals, democracy is not an end in itself, but an indispensable agency to secure liberty, individuality, and diversity. A contemporary problem in discussing liberalism is that the term is used differently in different countries. In Europe, and other parts of the world, liberalism is associated with free trade and limited government. In the United States, liberalism is contrasted with conservatism, and the term is applied in almost the opposite sense than in the rest of the world. As used in this book, liberalism conforms to the classical European definition.

The term "liberal" in liberal democracy refers to a particular form of democracy that adheres to the ideology of political liberalism. Liberal democracies feature constitutional protections of individual rights and universal suffrage. According to the principles of liberal democracy, the political process should be competitive with the participation of multiple and distinct political parties (political pluralism) and elections need to be free, frequent, and fair. Some liberal democracies also employ a vertical separation of powers (federalism) as an additional mechanism to increase public participation by delegating some governing powers to municipal and provincial governments. In short, a liberal democracy is, by definition and design, a governing system where power is not concentrated.

A key and necessary characteristic of democratic governance and culture is the concept of a "loyal opposition." Political competitors are loyal not to the specific policies of their competitors, but to the fundamental legitimacy of the state and to the democratic process itself. Political adversaries in a democracy share a common commitment to the democratic system. Political competitors may disagree vehemently, but must acknowledge the legitimate and essential roles that disagreement plays in the process. When the election is over, the judgment of the voters is accepted by all competitors, and the transfer of power proceeds peacefully. In a healthy democracy, political adversaries do not consider themselves lifelong enemies. Unfortunately, this critical distinction between an adversary and an enemy is one that does not pervade the Cuban disposition in general and Cuban politics in particular. More often than not, Cuban political processes have equated a political adversary with an enemy, with disastrous results for the nation.

Political philosopher Charles Montesquieu, famous for his articulation of the theory of separation of powers, argued, "Better it is to say, that the government most comfortable to nature is that which best agrees with the humor and disposition of the people in whose favor it is established." What program of governance best agrees with the "humor and disposition" of the Cuban nation is the topic of Chapter VI.

Chapter VI – Carajo, Somos como Somos (We Are the Way We Are)

The Difference
A Cuban teacher asks Pepito to explain to
the class what capitalism is. Pepito tells the
class that he thinks of it as a junkyard filled
with cars, food, and toys. "Very good," says
the teacher. "Now tell us what communism
is." Pepito answers, "It's the same junkyard,
except it is empty."

Political humor in Cuba

A NATION-STATE IS NOT A static phenomenon, and post-Castro Cuba
will need to rebuild much more than its economy; it will need to
rebuild its national identity. It cannot hope to do so, however, by
seeking to change fundamental characteristics of Cuban nationhood.
These reflections recognize that Cuban civil society has been decimated
by Castroism and has developed its own systemic characteristics and
perverse inner logic as a means of survival. Cuban civil society has
been drained of sociopolitical energy and the capacities of the citizenry
to take individual and collective responsibility for their lives have
been damaged. Thus, philosophically and pragmatically, post-Castro
Cuba needs to seek sociopolitical and economic policies targeted
towards individuals, and their fundamental character, not their current
dispositions. A starting point is to acknowledge a peculiar form of

libertarianism that manifests itself as habits of irreverence.

Even by the jovial standards of the Spanish-speaking Caribbean, Cubans stand out as inherently informal, irreverent, undisciplined, irrepressible, and fun-loving. Cuban folklore, replete with humor, asserts that Cubans can be forgiven for anything except for being *pesado* (roughly, fastidious or pedantic). Cuban writer and comedian Guillermo Alvarez Guedes has captured these Cuban traits brilliantly in his comedy routines. Cuban readers who may have grown up reading *Zig Zag*—a political humor weekly closed by Castro in the early days of the revolution—or listening to Leopordo Fernandez's (*Tres Patines*) hilarious radio show *La Tremenda Corte* can intuitively apprehend these idiosyncratic traits. In 1928, Cuban intellectual Jorge Mañach published a classic psycho-cultural analysis of these Cuban attitudes and behavior patterns under the title *La Indagación del Choteo* (inadequately translated as "An Investigation of Mockery"). Mañach defines and analyses the Cuban habits of irreverence, disrespectfulness, and repugnancy for all authority, and the disdain for hierarchy or rank (*jerarquia*). He posits that these traits reflect perhaps an inordinately high level of self-esteem and the prior failures of hierarchies in an individual social ambit.

These traits can be found even in the rarefied world of Cuban academics and scholarship. Cuban intellectuals can write and present works with rigorous and punctilious scholarly precision. But once the formal work is done, their collegial interchanges quickly turn to *choteo* and *jodedera*—peculiar forms of "messing with someone" that are mildly vulgar but not necessarily obscene. In religious matters, for example, Cubans practice Catholicism and other faiths *a mi manera* (my way), or Cuban style (*a la Cubana*). Religious syncretism is characteristic of Cuban worship. Some of these traits are not exclusively Cuban; an eccentric sociopolitical un-seriousness also permeates other Latin American cultures. Recently we have witnessed among Latin American presidents an incessant charlatan, a former Catholic bishop with a number of illegitimate children, and a president going on a hunger strike and sustaining himself by chewing coca leaves—not to mention (forgive the paralipsis) the debauchery of Cuban leaders.

In terms of governance, a first pass at these characteristics of the Cuban nation would suggest that Cubans are simply ungovernable. Alternatively, it would seem that Marxism-Leninism, with its doctrinal rigidity, would be the most appropriate paradigm to repress the natural disposition of Cubans. But fifty years of totalitarian rule puts to rest that notion. The new Cuban man has not emerged from Castroism. What sociopolitical and economic mores can be accessed by post-Castro Cuban leaders?

Efforts to capture the present value orientations and opinions of Cubans by examining those of recently arrived Cubans in Miami offer some insights.[67] As noted by Gomez and Rothe, studies of this genre seek to measure the value orientations of cultural groups by targeting various domains. For example: how the individual understands the character of human nature (good vs. evil vs. neutral); how the individual relates to authority (paternalistic vs. egalitarian vs. individualistic); how the individual orients himself with respect to time (tradition or past vs. present vs. future); how the individual chooses to use activity (pleasure vs. ambition vs. spirituality); how the individual relates to nature (subjugated by it vs. in harmony vs. subjugates it).

A selective overview of this study shows that a vast majority of recently arrived Cubans (96 percent) support a free market economy.[68] Fifty-three percent shared that they would prefer to spend their free time "trying to get as far as they can in life." Although this is consistent with immigrant groups that tend to be future oriented, it is atypical for people of Hispanic and Mediterranean origin, who place a higher value on relationships and enjoying the company of family and friends. In response to a question seeking to elicit how the participants would respond to personal financial difficulties, 65 percent responded that they would find a second job, and only 12 percent indicated that they would ask the government for help. In a clear demonstration of the

---

67   Gomez, Andy S. and Rothe, Eugenio M. "Value Orientations and Opinions of Recently Arrived Cubans in Miami." *ICCAS*. 2004.

68   Since these interviews were conducted with Cubans that had left the island (i.e., immigrants), the results may not be statistically presented as necessarily reflecting the views of the entire population.

distrust of government and the government controlled media, 0 percent of the respondents indicated that they used national newspaper and television as their source of reliable information while living in Cuba. When asked to report "the three most difficult issues they encountered while living in Cuba," the responses were: Unable to express one's true thoughts and opinions (78%), having limited options for the future (52%), and the lack of foods and other essentials (52%).

What is most readily discernible from these responses is that Cubans on the island have a high level of distrust for the communist institutions and authority. Although this sample may not be necessarily representative of the entire population on the island, recently arrived Cubans show a remarkable desire for individual free-market opportunities and advancement even after five decades of communism. After a lifetime of failed experimentations with collectivist approaches, Cubans may not know exactly how to achieve it, but they are ready for a dramatic break with their past.

The Cuban Post-Castro Interregnum

An interregnum is a period of discontinuity of government organization or social order. Traditionally, it represented the period of time between the reign of one monarch and the next. In the United States, the term may be applied to the period of time between the election of a new president and his inauguration, a period during which the outgoing president remains in power, but as a lame duck. The idea of an interregnum emphasizes the sequential relationship between what came before and what comes next.

Unfortunately, the Cuban transition to democracy and free markets is highly unlikely to follow the path of some of the most successful Eastern European countries that faced similar, but not identical challenges. Cuba's post-Castro interregnum will be, arguably, the most critical period in the nation's history. It will be a period during which inexperienced post-Castro Cuban leaders will face myriad social, political, and economic policy decisions. Unseasoned leaders will need to make strategic, tactical, and operational policy choices that will impact not only the existing circumstances, but the nation's immediate and long-term future. And, in all probability, this will have to take place in an environment of sociopolitical and economic disarray and confusion, if not outright chaos. They will need to avoid what Cuban author and intellectual Carlos Alberto Montaner, in a related context, labels as *"los viejos fantasmas y los nuevos peligros"* —the old ghosts and the new dangers.[69]

The full spectrum of social, political, and economic ideologies will be on display during this interregnum period and for years into the future. Reformers of all persuasions will compete for power and political influence. At one extreme will be the **reincarnation** or **continuity** "reformers" or government officials arguing for a relative status quo with only very gradual and tentative reforms, perhaps even under the auspices of the communist party or some successor. At the other extreme will be those seeking an abrupt and dramatic break with the past, a "shock therapy" of sorts, particularly in economic policies. In between will be a full range of Social Democratic and Christian Democratic approaches and much more. Superimposed on this process will be the exile community, the United States, and the international and global business communities. Among the new dangers will be democracy Cuban style (*a la Cubana*), or quite likely a proliferation of atomistic political parties approaching in number that of the Cuban adult population.

The question we are seeking to address in this chapter is limited to which of the modern political philosophies is best suited for the Cuban disposition. Other topics will be addressed in later chapters.

A starting point is to recognize fully that Cuba's centrally planned economy is simply not reformable in macroeconomic terms. It cannot be reformed gradually as in a Darwinian evolutionary process. To state categorically that Cuban Communism is not reformable is a shorthand expression to highlight that even minor reforms quickly become incompatible with the existing order of things. They become

---

69 Montaner, Carlos Alberto. *La Libertad y sus Enemigos.* Editorial Sudamérica. Buenos Aires 2005: p 13

unsustainable because they cannot coexist with the political and economic order.

It is also important to highlight that a reincarnation or continuity regime of the *cambiar para que todo siga igual* (change so that everything stays the same) tilt would be incapable of reforming itself. This type of regime in post-Castro Cuba, masquerading as a change agent, would not be able to repress in totalitarian fashion, nor would it be able to reform itself completely. It would have a very constricted scope of meaningful policy actions. Moreover, a rigid top-down command economy is antithetical to the disposition of the Cuban nation, where maxims like *Juro, pero no prometo* (I swear, but I will not promise), *Obedezco pero no cumplo* (I obey but I do not comply), and *a mi manera* (my way) prevail. Economic reforms constrained to the microeconomic domain of small businesses will not, by themselves, integrate Cuba's economy into the modern global economic system. In other words, a small isolated private sector economy geared for domestic production cannot sustain the economic development of the nation.

Most critical is the acknowledgement that Cuba's future economic and political systems must be grounded on the natural disposition of the Cuban nation. Just as important is the recognition that there is no messianic infinite wisdom that can efficiently organize a society from top to bottom. Socioeconomic and political efficiencies and effectiveness rest with the immeasurable number of small, atomistic choices made by empowered citizens. To unleash these governing efficiencies and effectiveness, a liberal philosophy of government, in the classical modern sense, offers the alternative. A philosophy of citizen empowerment is also the best suited for the national psyche and the values that now permeate the Cuban disposition. A philosophy of citizen empowerment would also allow the Cuban citizenry to begin the return to individual responsibility from the collectivist legacy of Castroism and to recapture individual energies. It addresses the high level of distrust for institutions and authority while allowing the necessary time for the rebuilding of a civil society.

Liberalism does not entail plans dictating goals for society. Its operational focus is on building institutions that liberate the creative forces of a nation, on governmental transparency and exemplary public administration. It is diametrically opposed to telling citizens how to organize and live their lives. In this sense, a liberal democracy will be "shock therapy" for the Cuban population accustomed to a litany of economic plans and government control over most aspects of their daily lives. Indeed, studies of societies transitioning from totalitarianism to democratic rule show that some individuals become confused and frustrated with how they are expected to respond to authority and initiative. But this is a fleeting condition and will disappear quickly, given the Cuban character.

In post-Castro Cuba, reliance on human capital is what will resonate with the irreverent Cuban nation and not prescribed, programmatic, rigid approaches to governance *somos como somos*—we are the way we are. If properly channeled with freedoms and empowerment, this Cuban trait offers a way to escape the ghosts of the past and navigate the dangers and challenges of the future.

None of this is to suggest that the dire situation with respect to Cuba's civil society and values, or the negative traits of the Cuban disposition (e.g., lack of respect for the law and institutions) discussed in earlier chapters will be immediately obliterated by liberal democracy. They will not. Nor is it the intention to compare and contrast the various alternatives to governance that will be considered during Cuba's interregnum. Those general topics have been debated ad nauseam for centuries and will not be settled here. The idea is not to offer some Pollyannaish view of liberal democracy, but to discuss how some of its workings fit the Cuban disposition and the needs of Cuban society. An accompanying central topic is the role of the market.

The Logic of the Market

The empirical evidence pointing to market-driven economies as the most effective and efficient wealth-creating systems is unambiguous. All of the wealthiest countries in the world rely on free market mechanisms. Private property and the rule of law are central to the economies of the developed countries. But why exactly is this the factual reality of an empirical world? Michael Sherner in *The Mind of the Market* aptly describes the how and whys of the market: "The market is the designspace of economics.[70] Just as nature selects the variation best suited to survive in a particular environment, so too do people select the goods and services that are best suited to meet their unique needs and desires in a particular market." In other words, social behavior and economics are not independent of each other. Rather, they are parts of a larger socioeconomic system in which people interact, process information, and adapt their behavior to changing conditions in innumerable ways. Markets are complex, interactive, and catalytic with an emphasis here on markets as a catalytic force capable of transforming post-Castro Cuba in complex social dimensions that exceed its role as a wealth-creating mechanism.

In some ways, we are remarkably irrational beings. We are driven by unconscious emotions that have evolved over millions of years, perhaps to a greater degree than by logic and conscious reason developed only a few seconds ago in evolutionary time. Behavioral economists have developed an experiment called the Ultimatum Game that serves to illustrate how social behavior and economic decisions interact with each other. The simplest variant of an Ultimatum Game is set up so that two players interact to decide how to divide a sum of money (e.g., $1,000). The money is given to the first player (she), who must offer to split the money with the second player (he). The first player proposes how to divide the sum between them, and the second player can either accept or reject this proposal. If the second player rejects, neither player receives anything. If the second player accepts, the money is split according to the proposal. The game is played only once and anonymously so that reciprocation is not an issue.

How much should a purely rational *homo economicus* offer? A relatively small amount, say, $100; an amount approaching a 50:50 split; or a generous $900? If the potential recipient of this windfall is a rational, self-interested *homo economicus,* he should clearly accept any offer, no matter how small (in Cuban terms, $100 would be

---

70 Shermer, Michael. *The Mind of the Market*. New York. Times Books, Henry Hold and Company, LLC. 2008.

equivalent to six months' salary). By rejecting a disproportional small offer of $100, the potential recipient is irrationally choosing nothing rather than something. He would be better off accepting any offer that enriches him by any amount whatsoever. Knowing this, the offering party should offer the smallest (non-zero) amount possible. As a *homo economicus*, she should seek to maximize her own monetary benefit.

Interestingly, in many cultures people offer "fair" splits approaching 50:50, and offers of less than 20 percent are often rejected. Researchers find that over 80 percent of the players in this anonymous, one-shot setting reject the approach of minimum money transfer and acceptance predicted by a pure rationality model. Proposals that move much below a 70:30 split are frequently rejected. Since individuals who reject a positive offer are electing to get nothing rather than something, they must not be acting solely to maximize economic gain. The classical explanation of the Ultimatum Game is that the economic model of self-interest is incomplete. Other explanations offer concerns with reputation, inequity aversion, or empathy models as possible explanations. Rejections in the Ultimatum Game are also due to adverse psychological reactions to stingy offers.

Keep in mind that in this basic version of the Ultimatum Game, there is only one party making an offer—one monopolistic supplier of goods and services—and the potential beneficiary is limited to a one-time, accept-or-reject choice. In our discussion, this is somewhat analogous to a totalitarian state with a command economy system. There are variables of the game that introduce alternatively proposer and responder competition, jointly called the "Competitive Ultimatum Game." In the Ultimatum Game with responder competition, there are four responders and one proposer. This is an even more accurate depiction of a totalitarian system with one producer (the state) and many responders (the citizenship). Each responder citizen can accept or reject an offer. Only one deal will be accepted, and the other responders get nothing. The state, now armed with the knowledge that it has several potential responder customers, each vying for its offer, has every incentive to make a lowball offer (something like $10) and retain the difference of $990, in our example. Indeed, this is precisely what happens in the Ultimatum Game with responder competition. Usually the proposer offers close to zero.

In contrast, the Ultimatum Game with proposer competition offers a variant in which there are four proposers (producers) all competing to get their offer accepted by a single responding customer. The responder can accept only one offer, and this winning offer represents the deal that will be carried out. The other three proposers get nothing. Amazingly, it turns out that with more than three proposers competing with each other, the responder (read: society) is offered almost the entire amount. In this exercise, the proposers will happily take the $10 "profit" and offer the remaining $990 rather than get nothing at all. This is not unlike what happens in a competitive free-market economy, where producers' net income tends to be in the single digits in most competitive industries. In the United States, for example, supermarket chains competing with many rivals tend to average net incomes in the low single digits. Such is the power and logic of the market.

The inanity of trying to control an entire economy is only matched by the inanity of trying to control human nature. As Shermer points out, only millions of buyers and sellers in constant real-time negotiation with millions of other buyers and sellers can determine the prices of the billions of products and services offered in a modern economy. In short, the economy is a product of human action and not of human design. Consequently, economies are best structured from the bottom up—consumer driven—and not from the top down—production driven.

Regrettably, market solutions to social problems are viewed negatively by advocates of a large role for government in the economy. In part this may be because we have a very low tolerance for economic ambiguity, and free markets are chaotic, uncertain, uncontrollable, and unpredictable. But it's mostly because free and fair markets require political states based on the rule of law, with property rights and independent legislative and judicial systems to formulate fair and just laws and to enforce those laws. These conditions are anathema to totalitarianism since, by definition, independent legislative and judicial systems dilute the prerogatives of the all-powerful state. The most effective and efficient politico-economic system yet devised is a liberal democracy with its attendant free market capitalism. It is this system of democratic-capitalism that leads to the greatest prosperity, the greatest liberty, and the greatest happiness for the greatest number.

If this is the case—and to restate, it is empirically unambiguous that it is—why do some governments continue to take pride in their high level of social expenditures? A partial answer is because, as noted above, market solutions to social problems are viewed with skepticism. There is also a fantasy that assigning a humanitarian task to the government, say healthcare, automatically imbues the entire process with an inherent effectiveness. These government tasks are supposed to correct market inefficiencies. The topic of market inefficiencies is another one of those that exceeds the scope of this book and is amply covered in the economic literature. But it is pertinent here to comment on the perverse logic of championing social expenditures as a fundamental "reason for being" of government.

Montaner highlights this perverse logic by noting that some individuals believe that the quality of a state should be measured by the amount of "social expenditures" that the state incurs.[71] The more the state spends on social subsidies, the more compassionate the state is believed to be. This logic reverses the terms. The funding for social expenditures must, of course, be obtained by relying on contributions from other sectors of society via taxation or other mechanisms. Wealth is not being created, just redistributed. The goal of the state should be to gradually reduce social expenditures to the point where they become unnecessary. This would signify that the socioeconomic systems in place have succeeded in creating circumstances under which all, or most, citizens are able to provide adequately for their own needs. Thus the quality of a state should be measured in inverse proportion to the social expenditures that are required to assists its citizens.

It should not be necessary, but perhaps it is, to make clear that there is nothing in this reasoning precluding the creation of basic social safety nets to allow all citizens a modicum of resources to compete in society. Also, it is typical at this point in any discussion of the role of the market and social policies that the examples of the Scandinavian

---

71 Montaner, Carlos Alberto. p 44

countries are brought up. The economies of those countries, unlike the economy of Cuba, are anchored on highly productive market-based systems.

In the Cuba of tomorrow, social expenditures must be intellectually repositioned as necessary but temporary, not as a permanent goal of the state. To accomplish this, it will also be necessary to discredit the mercantilist mythology that nations compete for a fixed amount of wealth in a sort of zero-sum game. Free markets are all about the creation of wealth. A pivotal role of a liberal democracy is to empower its citizens and to create the enabling conditions for citizens to recapture individual responsibility. Given the opportunity, Cubans in a post-Castro liberal democracy will be able to do just that. This has been amply demonstrated by the success of the Cuban Diaspora working and living in liberal democracies.

Chapter VII – Cuban Informality and Choice Architecture

All our knowledge falls within
the bounds of possible experience.

Immanuel Kant

IN HIS WORKS, DAMIAN FERNANDEZ describes aptly Cuban contempt for institutional norms (*lo informal*) and its corollaries for effective democratic governance. He notes that Cuban informality is not an explicitly articulated intellectual framework, but rather a pattern of behavior with its own logic, norms, vocabulary, economic rationality, and emotional infrastructure. "From the perspective of *lo informal*, the private is the basis for the public. It values the personal touch, the role of person-to-person contact, and the bonds of affection among family members and friends above the impersonal norms of the state."[72]

However, in and of itself, informality need not be thought of as necessarily caustic. Its social corrosiveness flows from its reliance on bending the rules and bypassing legal norms and on its capacity and effectiveness in securing benefits for the informal network. Bypassing legal norms to overcome the impersonal bureaucracies of ineffective government institutions immerses individuals into a culture of practicing illegality as a means of surviving. Cuban informality as a

---

72 Fernandez, Damian. p 11

mechanism to get things done (*para resolver*) accustoms individuals to ignore or break the law, and as such undermines institution building and respect for the rule of law. It is in this context that Cuban informality becomes an obstacle to a sustainable liberal democracy in post-Castro Cuba. The challenge, as Fernandez points out, is "how to translate the norms of *lo informal* into ones that help bind the individual into larger organizations and into community." More specifically for our consideration, how do Cubans create a sociopolitical and economic environment that can prosper in concordance with, or in spite of, this characteristic of Cuban culture?

For starters, Cuban proclivity for individualism and anti-institutionalism is intellectually concordant with a liberal philosophy of government. This is not to suggest that current Cuban attitudes, values, and behavioral patterns are conducive to building a civil society; not even close. Cuban informality is not a new phenomenon. Its roots can be traced to the colonial period, but it has been exacerbated by the demands to *resolver* (to make ends meet) imposed by the failed Cuban economic system. During the Castro period, Cubans have perfected a form of dual morality (*doble moral*) where one standard of conduct applies to the public sphere and a different one to private conduct. Neither pre-Castro Cuba, nor most countries in Latin America today, can be thought of as liberal societies. The right to vote and to freely elect leaders by itself does not constitute a liberal democracy. The reason for being of modern liberal democracies is to protect the civil liberties and political rights of the individual, including economic rights and liberties. An earlier claim that the Cuban system is not reformable by its governing elite is based, in part, on the fact that allowing private economic activities, even in a limited fashion, endangers the interests of the government bureaucracy. The private sector grows spontaneously and often much more than anticipated by the authorities seeking to control its activities. The inherent contradiction manifests itself in various ways, of which *lo informal* and the black market are classic examples.

One way to think about this topic is to come to appreciate that a liberal democracy in post-Castro Cuba is not a panacea. It is an absolutely necessary but insufficient condition. It will provide the playing field in which newly empowered citizens can pursue their individual goals. But it will be unsustainable if it is undermined by disrespect for democratic institutions and the rule of law. A liberal democracy offers the best antidote for the pathological condition of anti-institutionalism, but it must be formulated to work for individuals and perceived as such.

Notwithstanding its solid theoretical and experiential underpinnings, a liberal democracy will not receive the support of the population and will not be defended by the citizenry if it does not prove to be beneficial in their day-to-day lives. Only if a liberal democracy is perceived to be convenient and in the best interest of individual goals can it counteract the worst anti-institutional aspects of Cuban informality. Informality and anti-institutionalism are persistent and pervasive conditions in Cuban society precisely because they work well as responses to government inefficiency and corruption. In short, they deliver benefits. The respect for democratic institutions and the rule of law will come about over time only if they prove to be a more effective and abundant source of benefits than its "informality" alternative.

This requires Cuban leaders to understand that to govern is not to command. To govern is to manage wisely and with respect for the rule of law the monies and resources provided by the citizenry. The proclivity for anti-institutionalism is one of the many obstacles to a sustainable liberal democracy in Cuba. It is a resistant condition, but not an unassailable one. Our empathic nature is the basis for a civil society. In Cuban culture, that empathic nature seeks to address family distress *resolviendo* by bending the rules. But if instead that family distress can be addressed better by following the rules, then Cuban civil society can be rebuilt on the foundation of our empathic nature.

Cuban Informality: Necessary or Contingent?

In more formal terms, the proposition is one of distinguishing between what happens necessarily and what happens contingently. The most negative characteristics of Cuban informality are not inherently necessary. They are contingent. They have become necessary mostly as a means to an end. A functioning liberal democracy begins the process of returning *lo informal* to the realm of the contingent.

If, as argued above, the contempt Cubans display for institutional norms is a contingent condition, then the challenge turns to the operational questions of policymaking. Clearly, priorities are in the realms of education and institution building. Education and institutions for the protection of economic rights and liberties are particularly critical in the context of the current discussion. Independent judicial and legislative branches and their attendant operational institutions are essential. Corruption at all levels must be fought vigorously. Issues regarding unresolved property settlements must be addressed, transitional social safety nets must be put in place, and much more. But as we have learned in nation-building efforts throughout the world, it is much easier to build new parliament or justice buildings than to populate those buildings with legislators and justices committed to democratic governance and the rule of law.

The development of civic skills and civic virtues will require more than classroom learning and more than the opportunity to practice those skills in the playing field provided by a liberal democracy. Civic education is a long-term process that will require generations to modify Cuba's political culture. In some cases (post-Castro Cuba being one) a functional liberal democracy, even with all its trimmings and attendant institutions, will require a gentle nudge to take hold. After five decades of indoctrination and demagoguery, Cubans will not respond to political exhortations; more creative approaches will be needed. One of the legacies of Castrosim is that Cubans will need to be nudged toward decisions that will improve their lives by making them more law-abiding citizens.

Nudging Cubans to Embrace Civic Values

Behavioral scientist and economist Richard Thaler and Cass Sunstein, professor of jurisprudence, both at the University of Chicago, have coauthored a provocative book titled *Nudge*.[73] The discussion here follows closely and borrows unabashedly from the authors' presentation and examples in the spirit that it is best to let the proponents of a novel concept speak for themselves.[74] Moreover, given the prescriptive emphasis on liberalism espoused in this work as Cuba's future philosophy of governance, it is essential to borrow the authors' words in defense and justification for their near-oxymoronic concept of "libertarian paternalism" as well as the application of "choice architecture." The only claim to originality here rests with the application of libertarian paternalism and choice architecture as tools to overcome the most negative characteristics of Cuban informality being considered.

It is well known, from the experiences of designing supermarket floor plans and the display of product choices, that small changes in the presentation context will influence which products will be purchased. For example, product manufacturers gladly pay location premiums to have their products displayed at eye level rather than on the bottom shelves. It has been demonstrated empirically that products displayed at eye level or in other more visible locations are purchased more frequently than those harder to see and reach. A supermarket choice architect thus has the responsibility for organizing the context in which people make their decisions over product choices. With this in mind, let's consider first a benign example for a societal application of choice architecture that even libertarians should not find objectionable.

Suppose that in an elementary school cafeteria food line, offerings are arranged at random, and that children, being children, overwhelmingly choose candy bars and other unhealthy food choices over healthy foods like apples for dessert. If society believes that it is in the best interest of these children to be nudged somehow to increase their consumption of healthy foods and decrease consumption of unhealthy items, is it legitimate to use choice architecture to arrange the food offerings

---

73 Thaler, Richard H and Sunstein, Cass R. *Nudge: Improving Decisions about Health, Wealth, and Happiness.* New Haven. Yale University Press. 2008

74 For expository ease, this discussion will not follow the rigorous academic protocols of explicitly quoting and referencing every borrowed sentence. The interested reader is referred to Thaler and Sunstein's excellent book.

so that children are more likely to select the healthier items? Does it offend our libertarian sensitivities to paternalistically place the candy bars at the end of the line? Is displaying the apples attractively and in a location that is easier to see and reach than the candy bars an egregious intrusion on free-choice principles? Notice that candy bars are not forbidden; all choices are left in place. The choice architecture here is limited to focusing the children's attention in a particular direction, not on restricting their choices.

Speaking of focusing attention, let's consider next a wonderful example of this subliminal nudging principle offered by Thaler and Sunstein. It seems that when men use public urinals, they usually do not pay much attention to where they aim. If they see a target, attention, and therefore accuracy, is dramatically improved. In the men's restrooms at Schiphol Airport in Amsterdam, authorities have etched the image of a black housefly into each urinal. It appears that when men see a target, they aim at it—greatly improving their aim. Authorities have conducted fly-in-urinal trials (really) that show that the fly etchings reduce spillage by 80 percent. Choice architecture, before it had a fancy name, has been a steady feature in our daily lives. Doctors describing the alternative treatments available to a patient, printers designing a form that new employees fill out to enroll in a company's health plan, parents describing possible educational choices to their children, and marketing specialists are all choice architects.

Thaler and Sunstein take pains to point out that the libertarian aspect of their proposed strategies rests in the insistence that, in general, people should be free to do what they prefer and also free to opt out of undesirable arrangements if they want to. Their aim is to design policies that maintain or increase freedom of choice. The paternalistic aspect lies in the claim that it is legitimate for choice architects to try to influence people's behavior in order to make their lives longer, healthier, and better. They argue for self-conscious efforts by institutions in the private and public sectors to steer people's choices in directions that will improve their lives. The emphasis is in influencing choices in a way that will improve people's lives *as judged by themselves*. They define nudging as efforts to alter people's behavior without forbidding any options or significantly changing their economic incentives. To count as a nudge, the intervention must be easy and cheap to avoid. Placing the apples at eye level in the cafeteria food line counts as a nudge; banning junk food does not.

The most immediate criticism is, of course, that these influences may be exercised for benevolent or nefarious purposes—for better or worse. Libertarians (and some liberals), please hold your fire for a few more pages. There are no perfect solutions, and at times society must choose the less toxic and damaging options available. Consider that if incentives and nudges replace requirements and bans, government will be both smaller and more modest. For the most part, well-designed nudges are not intrusive or coercive, they cost little or nothing, and they impose no burden on taxpayers. Even if by magic or some act of Divine Providence, Cuba *mañana* finds itself with an *ipso facto* liberal democracy, it will be a sort of proto-liberal democracy unlikely to meet the ideal standards or the expectations of most liberal intellectuals. Cuban society will need to be nudged in the direction of modern civil society.

Can the approaches and techniques of choice architecture be used in post-Castro Cuba to counter the "status quo bias" and the worst aspects of *lo informal* and Cuban anti-institutionalism? Should they be employed? Who gets to decide the direction of nudging? Is this a slippery slope toward more sophisticated forms of state control? The positive answer to the first question is yes. As Thaler and Sunstein show with many examples in different spheres, choice architecture and the emerging science of choice offer infinite applications. The normative answers to the other questions are much trickier and require some more elaboration.

Any post-Castro Cuban government (particularly of the **reincarnation** or **continuity** genre), and society in general, will experience the condition of status quo bias (a fancy name for inertia). The status quo bias will manifest itself in governance, perhaps in the reluctance to undertake rapid political reforms, in the formulation of economic policymaking, in the dismantling of communist institutions, and most pertinently for the present focus, inertia in replacing a culture of *lo informal* with a reliance on institutions and the rule of law. Generally, individuals make good choices in the contexts in which they have experience, good information, and prompt feedback. They do less well in contexts in which they are inexperienced and poorly informed, and in which feedback is slow or infrequent. We can all choose among ice cream flavors with little difficulty. We know what we like, we know the choices available (e.g., chocolate, vanilla), and we have had experience with the various flavors. Our taste buds provide immediate feedback. On the other hand, if we are asked to choose from a large number of prescription drug plans, all with multiple and varying features, we are likely to welcome a little help in determining which plan best serves our needs.

Technically, if people are not choosing perfectly, *as judged by their own preferences,* choice architecture and nudging protocols will be valuable tools. Even if liberal democracy offers an ample playground in which to exercise liberties, Cubans on the island have had little experience with such liberties. They will be skeptical of any government generated information, and the feedback they will receive from law-abiding civil conduct will not offer immediate positive feedback. Without a little nudging, the tried and tested alternative of "bending the rules" behavior will prevail. It will reflect their status quo bias.

Chapter VI introduced *homo economicus* as the rational, self-serving being that is the foundation of classical economics. It was shown with the Ultimatum Game that the self-serving model is incomplete if it fails to account that, as *homo sapiens,* our behavior is not always purely rational. One explanation offered by psychologists and neuroscientists, and more recently adopted by economists, is that our decision making process involves two kinds of thinking: one that is intuitive and automatic, and another that is reflective and rational. So that the discussion does not stray too far, it will be limited here to the main topic at hand—the law-bending, anti-institutional Cuban proclivities. To illustrate, most Americans have an Automatic System reaction to a temperature given in Fahrenheit, but have to use their Reflective System to process a temperature given in Celsius; for Europeans, the opposite is true. As Thaler and Sunstein explain it, the Automatic System is our gut reaction, and the Reflective System is our conscious thought. The Automatic System of Cubans on the island starts with having no idea how to conduct oneself as responsible law-abiding citizens in a liberal democracy. Their gut reactions and predispositions will be to rely on the proven success of *lo informal.* If the United States were to adopt the metric system tomorrow, retraining the Automatic Systems of Americans to think in Celsius would take considerable time and effort; likewise for the development of civic virtues and responsibilities in post-Castro Cuba.

Consider also that, *grosso modo,* losing something makes us twice as miserable as gaining the same thing makes us happy. That is to say, people are "loss averse." Loss aversion is but one of the reasons for the status quo bias. A key principle of choice architecture is that this status quo bias can be readily manipulated. Simply put, Cubans, as all humans, are "nudge-able." The current default pattern of behavior of Cubans is bending the rules to *resolver.* But that behavior pattern can be influenced or nudged toward law-abiding behavior. Two additional examples from Thaler and Sunstein should suffice to illustrate the practical applications of choice architecture and nudging.

Undisputedly, it is in the best interest of society at large that individuals save during their working lives so that they can adequately meet their financial needs in retirement. The fact that many people do not save for retirement exacerbates the social security safety net systems in many countries. In response, in the United States, for example, the government has implemented legislature to encourage personal savings. Tax-favored saving accounts such as 401(k) programs are well intentioned and offer significant financial incentives. Corporate contributions to 401(k) programs are tax deductible, gains are tax deferred, and in many plans, employers match at least a part of the employee contributions. For *homo economicus,* this should be a no-brainer. And yet, as *homo sapiens,* many Americans who are eligible for such plans do not take full advantage of them. Roughly 30 percent of employees eligible to join 401(k) plans fail to enroll. In some cases, it may be sensible not to join (e.g., workers with other pressing financial needs), but in most cases non-enrollment is a case of status quo bias. Normally, it requires a little effort to enroll in a 401(k) plan when the default condition is non-enrollment. When the employee is first eligible to enroll, they have to fill out an enrollment form, then they must decide how much money to put aside and how to allocate their savings among the investment vehicles offered in the plan.

What happens if the default condition is nudged so that the employee is automatically enrolled in the company's 401(k) plan? (Typically, automatic enrollment programs adopt a relatively low default savings rate of 2 or 3 percent, and a very conservative investment choice). What happens if the employee is automatically enrolled unless he or she actively fills out a simple form asking to opt out? One study showed participation rates of barely 20 percent after three months of employment when the default was that the employee had to opt in. When automatic enrollment was adopted as the default condition and employees had to overcome their inertia to opt out, enrollment of new employees jumped to 90 percent.

Let's consider one last example of choice architecture principles at work to illustrate its myriad societal applications before returning to its applicability in post-Castro Cuba.

Thaler and Sunstein note when introducing a one-chapter discussion of this thought-provoking topic that it deserves an entire book. Necessarily, all the complexities and moral issues will be ignored in this brief three-paragraph treatment. Organ transplants save and improve thousands of lives each year. Eighty percent of organ donations come from deceased donors. Unfortunately, the demand for organs greatly exceeds the supply. At any given time, tens of thousands of Americans are on various waiting lists for organs. It is estimated that as many as 60 percent die while waiting for organ availability, and the waiting list is growing at a rate of 12 percent per year. The standard economic solution to this dilemma is permitting a market in organs; that discussion alone would be another book. Is there an application of choice architecture that can increase the availability of organ donations?

The primary sources of organs are patients that have been declared "brain dead." That is, they have suffered an irreversible loss of all brain function and are being sustained temporarily by artificial means. In the United States, approximately fifteen thousand potential donors each year are pronounced brain dead. Fewer than 50 percent become donors. The main obstacle to increasing donations is the requirement of obtaining the consent of surviving family members. Most states in the

U.S. apply an explicit consent rule when it comes to organ donations. Individuals have to take some concrete steps to demonstrate that they want to be organ donors. They have to opt in. Studies show that many who express their desire to become organ donors if tragic circumstances arrive fail to take the necessary action to document their desire by registering as organ donors. Explicit consent is the default rule and the status quo bias works against the desires of potential organ donors. As in other domains, the default rule and inertia work to contravene the expressed wishes of potential donors.

What happens if the default rule is changed from explicit consent to one of presumed consent? Under presumed consent, individuals would be presumed to be consenting donors; of course, they would have the opportunity to easily opt out and register their unwillingness to be donors. Some countries in Europe have adopted presumed consent laws, with an enormous impact on the consent rates of organ donations. Two similar countries, Austria and Germany, have presumed consent and explicit consent respectively. Austria's organ donor consent rate is 99 percent; Germany's is 12 percent. It is left to the readers and the ethicists to debate the pros and cons of changing the default rule for organ transfers.

Thaler and Sunstein conclude their book by arguing that seemingly small features of social situations can have massive effects on the behavior of individuals. They note that nudges are everywhere in society, even if we do not notice them, and that choice architecture, both good and bad, is pervasive and unavoidable. Their claim is that libertarian paternalism is not an oxymoron. Choice architects can preserve freedom of choice while also nudging individuals in directions that will improve their lives. It may be added, as will be developed in later chapters, that choice architecture can also be used to nudge leaders and policymakers themselves in the direction of better, more transparent, and more responsible governance.

Hopefully it is also clear to the readers that the point of offering these examples is not to advocate for the etchings of flies in Cuban urinals or to make all Cubans into organ donors. The goal is simply to introduce and illustrate the principles of choice architecture and suggest that the development of a culture of civic values and skills may be accelerated in post-Castro Cuba, with the help of some gentle nudging techniques. Sustaining a liberal democracy in post-Castro Cuba will be difficult at best. A civil society will not just emerge with the adoption of democracy and a free market. In 1787, at the close of the American Constitutional Convention in Philadelphia, a Mrs. Powel who anxiously awaited the results asked Benjamin Franklin, "Well, Doctor, what have we got, a republic or a monarchy?" "A republic if you can keep it," responded Franklin.

Cubans in post-Castro Cuba will need a little help in keeping their new government. Such is the legacy of Castroism. They will need some gentle nudging to adopt the rule of law as their Automatic System response. Choice architecture offers hope that the negative civic proclivities can be overcome if its techniques are consciously imbedded in private and public policymaking. Hope that if nudging is built into day-to-day choices, democracy will stay on track; hope that Cubans will not, as they have done so often in the past, opt out mentally or physically of a genuine transition. Let's hope.

Chapter VIII – The Pursuit of Happiness

Un caballero sólo defiende causas perdidas.

Jorge Luis Borges

IT IS AN OLD DEBATE. Before Thomas Jefferson penned one of the most famous phrases in the American Declaration of Independence, writing that we are endowed with "certain unalienable rights, that among these are Life, Liberty and the pursuit of Happiness," English philosopher John Locke had expressed that "no one ought to harm another in his life, liberty, or possessions." Jefferson's substitution for "possessions" or property with "the pursuit of Happiness" was not without objections then, and continues to be discussed today. As it turns out, not only are property rights essential for a nation's economic growth and development, but it appears they are also essential for the pursuit of happiness.

Studies consistently show that wealth does not equal happiness. Although individuals with higher incomes report higher levels of happiness and life satisfaction than those with lower incomes, the differences are small. Surprisingly, variations in income, education, occupation, gender, marital status, and other demographic characteristics explain little of the variations in people's reported level of subjective well-being. This persistent finding is often explained in terms of "aspiration adjustment" and "set point" models. These models postulate the following: (1) Recent life changes, such as receiving a raise or promotion (or negatively, losing one's job), can have a major impact on an individual's well-being, but people's aspirations quickly adjust to their level of achievement. After twelve months or so, individuals report the same level of well-being as they did before the change. They return to the individual's normal "set point." (2) Researchers believe that set points are genetically influenced and individual to each person.[75]

It turns out that what brings people the most happiness are social bonds (marriage, friendship, social circle), trust in people (friends, family, and strangers), trust in society (the economy, justice, government), religion and spirituality (prayer, meditation, positive psychology), and pro-social behavior (helping others, aiding the needy, volunteering). These are conditions that are fundamentally absent in a totalitarian regime, particularly in Cuba, where a distrustful and cynical citizenry unable to survive on the honest product of its labor routinely engages in illegalities, egoism, untruthfulness, and a general degradation of values. Michael Shermer in *The Mind of the Market* defines happiness as "an evolved emotion that guides us to find meaning in the simple social pleasures of interacting with our immediate family and extended family, friends, and social circle, and to direct us to find joy in the meaningful purposes of life that most directly involve helping ourselves, our family, our friends and our community."[76] He adds that research studies on international happiness and freedom show that "an increase in personal autonomy and self-control leads to greater happiness, and that people tend to be happier in societies with greater levels of individual autonomy and freedom compared to those in more totalitarian and collective systems."[77] In short, the pursuit of happiness in post-Castro Cuba requires the unleashing of the aspirations of all Cubans in an institutional, social, and politico-economic environment

---

75 Inglehart, Ronald and Klingemann, Hans-Dieter. "Genes, Culture, Democracy, and Happiness." in E. Diener and E. M. Suh (eds) *Culture and Subjective Well-Being*, pp. 165-183. Cambridge, MA: MIT Press. 2000.

76 Shermer, Michael. Kindle location 3159-66.

77 Shermer, Michael. Kindle location 4680.

that maximizes within-group amity and minimizes between-group enmity.

A parenthesis, before continuing with the present topic: The understanding of "aspiration adjustment" and set points helps to explain how Cubans adjusted their set points to the incremental misery of Castroism. Most importantly, it offers guidance for the future. A key lesson learned from the transition experiences of the former Soviet Union countries is that reform governments must act very quickly to implement profound reforms. The political window of opportunity for a transition government is short; perhaps no more than the one year that studies suggest it takes individuals to return to their set points. The interregnum post-Castro government will have a short-lived political honeymoon in which to set in motion the transformation of the country.

Traditionally, most studies of well-being have been conducted within a given society. Interestingly, responses to questions such as "How satisfied are you with your life as a whole?" show relatively little variation over time within a given country. For example, in the United States, consistently only a small minority describe themselves as unhappy or dissatisfied with their lives. This situation changes when researchers begin to examine cross-national variations. In virtually all advanced industrial societies, at least three-fourths of the population reports being either "very happy" or "fairly happy." But this is not the case for the rest of the world. As reported by Inglehart and Klingemann, cross-national variation in subjective well-being is strongly linked with the society's level of economic development.[78] Wealth may not make us happy, but it increases our personal life choices and impacts our sense of well-being as defined by researchers. Prosperity has an effect on human happiness, but most important is the societal trust that enables individuals to do what most directly helps themselves, their families, friends, and community.

---

78 Inglehart, Ronald and Klingemann, Hans-Dieter. "Genes, Culture, Democracy, and Happiness." in E. Diener and E. M. Suh (eds) *Culture and Subjective Well-Being*, pp. 165-183. Cambridge, MA: MIT Press. 2000.

In post-Castro Cuba, the transition from what is basically a subsistence economy to moderate economic security will have an initial large impact on happiness and life satisfaction. But, not unlike the life change of getting a raise or a promotion, people's aspirations will quickly adjust and return to their normal set point. Moreover, studies show that after a certain point, economic growth no longer makes a difference in perceived well-being. Inglehart and Klingemann note that practically all societies that experienced communist rule show relatively low levels of subjective well-being, even when compared with societies at a much lower economic level. The level of the subjective well-being of a society is closely related to the legitimacy of the country's socioeconomic and political system.

The question of the government's legitimacy will be crucial in post-Castro Cuba. Over time, Cubans will endow the institutions of a new government with legitimacy only if their lives have gone comparatively well under the new polity. In post-Castro Cuba, the much-needed flourishing of democratic institutions will be closely linked with the society's level of subjective well-being. Democracy and well-being are strongly linked, but the causal relationship is not a simplistic assumption that democratic institutions make people happy. In the end, the pursuit of happiness requires both the civil liberties and political freedoms of a liberal democracy as well as the economic prosperity of a free-market economy.

This argues for a reform process in Cuba that is broad-based, comprehensive, and carried out expeditiously, as opposed to a program of gradualist reforms. To enjoy the living standards and well-being of developed nations, it is necessary to also adopt their patterns of civic conduct. With this in mind, the next four chapters will focus on particular areas of reforms, e.g., personnel, institutions, politics, and economics. The emphasis will not be on precise disciplinary approaches, but on overall strategic considerations. Overlaying the subject-specific considerations is the notion that it is the Cuban people who must "buy into" the reforms. It is the Cuban people who must believe that, this time, the institutions will work for them rather than for the politicians. The country's socioeconomic and political systems and its institutions will not be legitimized unless they are perceived as helpful to personal happiness and life satisfaction. In other words, the philosophical and theoretical constructs we have been discussing will be far less important than the practical results.

Cubans in post-Castro society will not become law-abiding citizens just because new socioeconomic and political systems may be put in place. A brain drain of the country's best and brightest will not be avoided with exhortations to remain in Cuba for the reconstruction of the homeland. Appeals for patience will be ignored if transparency does not prevail and systemic corruption is not avoided. In post-Castro Cuba, the pursuit of happiness, in abeyance for fifty years, will intensify as opportunities become more visible and palpable. It will take place either in Cuba or elsewhere if conditions on the island are not conducive to personal economic growth. This preference for leaving the country is vividly captured in a statement by a recent Cuban immigrant: "We have been trying to build socialism for fifty years and failed miserably. I am not going to stay around to try to build capitalism for another fifty years. I want to live in a ready-made society."[79]

A key goal of this "happiness" discussion has been to highlight that as we seek to diminish the sorrow or grief that we feel at other's suffering we attenuate our own distress and bring out our positive qualities. And while much has been said about the deplorable state of Cuba's civil society, no satisfying quick-acting prescriptions have been offered. A starting point is to recognize that our empathetic nature is the key building block of a civil society. In order for Cuba to achieve prosperity and happiness as a nation, it is essential to maximize positive social interactions in an open marketplace of goods and ideas that increases trust in society and awakens our empathic nature. Only then can civil society begin to flourish.

---

79 Statement to the Institute for Cuban and Cuban American Studies, University of Miami, during interview with a group of Cuban immigrants.

Temporary Inexperience vs. Permanent Obstructionism

The story goes that in 1989, at the beginning of his presidency, Václav Havel, one of the principal protagonists of the Czech Republic's Velvet Revolution, was asked why he was substituting members of the previous government with new personnel. He responded, "Because I prefer temporary inexperience to permanent sabotage." One fundamental reason why Cuban communism is not gradually reformable is that, by definition, the principles of separation of powers are inimical to the interests of the nomenklatura. In a genuine transition, the ruling elite fears its institutional extinction and the disappearance or dilution of its privileges.

The Cuban nomenklatura has a built-in negative incentive towards democratic reforms. For instance, in order for property rights to be lawfully assured, an independent judiciary must be in place to adjudicate disputes according to the rule of law. Again, by definition, an independent judicial system based on the rule of law delimits the prerogatives of the ruling elite. Just laws not only deter corruption, but they also help to create a society in which individuals can preserve human dignity without recourse to corrupt practices, or in Cuban terms, without recourse to *la doble moral.* Without just laws and its attendant institutions, the burden of upholding the principles of justice falls on the individual citizens.

Corruption in government has a detrimental multiplier effect on society as a whole. In modern ethics, integrity has to do with the perceived consistency of actions, values, and principles. Integrity is the quality of having a sense of truthfulness with respect to the motivations for one's actions, that is, acting according to one's beliefs and values at all times. Integrity is also a refusal to engage in behavior that evades responsibility.

One of the most traumatic legacies of Castroism is that it has compromised the integrity of an entire nation. Individual citizens and government officials alike have not been free to act according to their beliefs and values. Incongruency between personal conduct and beliefs permeates society, challenging its moral wholeness. This existential angst originated with corruption from the top down and must be addressed the same way. If dishonesty in governance has a ripple effect on society, in some measure, the opposite must also be true for honesty in government. Václav Havel was probably wise in relying on a new team of committed and enthusiastic, albeit inexperienced, reformers to carry out his reform program to avoid the status quo bias. But, if the Cuban transition proceeds, more or less, along the expected **reincarnation** or **continuity** paths, the status quo bias will be fully in place.

On the other hand, it will be argued that wholesale changes of government officials can have catastrophic results, as shown by the United States' experience in Iraq, where Paul Bremer, the head of the U.S.-led civilian administration in Iraq, elected to dismantle Saddam's military and dissolve his Baath Party and other institutions in favor of a fresh new beginning. In post-Castro Cuba, the *tabula rasa* or blank-slate approach to the rebuilding of the country is replete with perils. So is the potential for permanent obstructionism that preoccupied Václav Havel. This is the first governing dilemma that will be faced by a Cuban transition government. As of this writing, it is hard to visualize a Cuban transition that proceeds in a straight line from Castroism to a liberal democracy. It is just as hard to visualize how a law-abiding civil society can evolve almost *ex nihilo* if a continuity type of transition prevails.

In the universe of political values, the planets that revolve around the sun of liberal democracy are liberty; personal freedoms; private property; equality before the law; checks and balances; free, fair, and frequent elections; pluralism; transparency; decentralization; tolerance; individual responsibility; rule of law; free markets; free enterprise; competency; meritocracy; prosperity; progress; and all their respective orbiting moons. It is only when functioning within a democratic system that politicians are likely to adjust to the perceptions and beliefs of those who elected them. The values universe of Cuba's nomenklatura and the legacy of Castroism do not include many (or any) of the above planets. Their ways of comprehending and apprehending reality reside in a different universe.

To illustrate why the universe of values of both the citizenship and the nomenklatura involves a different way of comprehending and apprehending reality, it may be useful to recall Plato's Allegory of the

Cave. Plato imagines a group of people (surely they were Cubans) who have lived all their lives chained in a cave facing a blank wall. All they are able to see are the shadows projected on the wall of people and animals passing in front of the cave entrance. To these cave prisoners, the shadows they see represent reality. It is all they have known, it is all they have experienced, and it is all they have ever seen. They have no idea, and no way of understanding, that the shadows on the wall (their lives under Castroism) do not constitute reality at all. What they take to be real is in fact an illusion.

An insidious legacy of Castroism is that all Cubans will struggle to see reality beyond their illusions. This condition will have manifold manifestations in civic life and in governance. Democracy is not an inevitable condition for Cuba, nor is it a lost cause. To paraphrase the Borges epitaph quoted at the beginning of this chapter, lost causes are the purview of gentlemen.

The purging methods totalitarian regimes use to refresh their leadership ranks are a case in point of this different way of perceiving reality. Political purges along Stalinist lines have been a feature of Castroism from the early days of the revolution, including the imprisonment of historical revolutionary figures like Comandante Huber Matos, the so-called battles against sectarianism and micro-factions in the 1960s, the indictments of high-level functionaries and military officials like the youth leader Luis Orlando Dominguez (1987), generals Arnaldo Ochoa and José Abrantes, minister Diocles Torralba (1989), ideologist Carlos Andana (1992), former foreign minister Roberto Robaina (1999), and more recently the purging of former favorites Carlos Lage and Felipe Pérez Roque (2009).

The octogenarian and near-octogenarian Cuban leadership of the Castro brothers and their presumed successors, historical revolutionaries Machado Ventura and Ramiro Valdez, represent the continuity scenarios, including political purges as the preferred mechanisms for regime renewal and personnel changes. Their political values universe is incompatible with the values of a liberal democracy. They simply do not subscribe to the notion that their replacements should be freely and competitively elected by the Cuban people. In terms of Cuba's political future, they are not "nudgeable." But biology will continue its inexorable course, and a new generation of Cuban leaders will eventually assume power. Most likely, they too will be continuity minded, but perhaps "nudgeable."

It is at this time that the gentlemen of Borges' lost causes must take up the Cuban cause. It is in the post-Castros-Machado-Valdez interregnum that the Cuban opposition, the exile community, the United States, and the international community must broker and engage in a negotiations process with the new leadership generation. Negotiations should be almost single mindedly focused on conducting a free and fair pluralistic electoral process. Only then can a genuine transition, not simply a succession, begin in Cuba. Part 2 of this work turns to some subject-specific challenges that will be faced *mañana* in Cuba.

Part Two

The Reform Process

Chapter IX – Personnel Reforms

When there are many men without
decorum, there are always others
who themselves possess the decorum
of many men.

José Marti

FOR HALF A CENTURY, THE prevailing wisdom, at least in the Cuban exile community, was that the demise of Fidel Castro would mean the end of communism in Cuba and that democracy would inevitably follow. That scatological vision of Cuban communism proved to be wildly inaccurate. The February 2008 succession from Fidel to Raul, programmed since the early days of the Revolution, was efficient, effective and seamless. However, given Raul Castro's age and possible health problems, there will be another succession in the not-too-distant future. José Ramon Machado Ventura, also elderly, is the perfunctory successor to Raul Castro. Similarly, Ramiro Valdez, a historical Comandante and contemporary of the Castros, is waiting in the wings. But neither of these men is obligatorily seen as Cuba's next leader in the same way that Fidel had anointed his younger brother as his successor. Perhaps an interesting parallel can be made with the events in the Soviet Union following Leonid Brezhnev's death in 1982. His 78-year-old successor, Yuri Andropov, died two years later. He was in turn succeeded by the also elderly Constantin Chernenko, who died a year after and was succeeded by Mikhail Gorbachev.

The next succession or two in Cuba may not go as smoothly as the one from Fidel to Raul, but it is highly unlikely, given the identified potential successors, that it will provide fertile ground for a genuine transition. Of course, the imponderable, the possibility of a black swan event is always present, but a legitimate transition may have to wait for a post-Castros-Machado-Valdez interregnum.[80] Also, as argued throughout this book, post-Castro does not mean the end of Castroism or its legacy.

It is in this particular interregnum that the opportunities for an authentic transition to democracy may arise. Crystal balling exercises suggest that it will have to be a negotiated transition process. At least initially, it will be essentially a top-down process. This is because the new generation of leaders will, in all probability, come from the Cuban Armed Forces (FAR). The Cuban military controls all major industries, is the most professional organization in the country, and, of course, has the firepower. In short, it is the only game in town. Unless there is a Václav Havel in their midst who is able to emerge and consolidate power as a true reformer, the new government will hold a status quo bias. Simply put, inertia offers greater personal benefits and security. It is important to clarify here that the precise sequence of events, their timing, or the names of the individual players is unpredictable and falls in the realm of speculation. For purposes of the discussion that follows, it is not essential to predict an exact sequence of events or to identify the protagonists. This particular post-Castro interregnum scenario may include instability, uncertainty, and much more. The point is simply that at some time, perhaps following a couple of iterations or false starts, a negotiating process must ensue if post-Castro Cuba is to undertake a peaceful transition.

Figuratively speaking, at the negotiating table will be the new leadership generation of governing officials and its constituencies, the Cuban opposition and citizenry, the exile community, the United States, and the international community. The Cuban opposition and the Cuban people will bring as their main bargaining chip the full

---

80 For expository convenience, post-Castro will be used now more explicitly to mean the eventual succession to a younger generation of leaders.

arsenal of peaceful civil disobedience mechanisms and pressure tactics (e.g., labor strikes, public demonstrations). The exile community will bring its institutional memory and the experiences and professional and financial resources accumulated while living, learning, working, and thinking in freedom. But the crucial role in brokering and engaging the new leadership generation in a negotiations process will have to be played by the international community, including the United States. It is only the international community that can access the supranational incentives and disincentives, the carrots and sticks, which will be necessary to broker a return to democratic rule. It is also the international community that will have to oversee that free and fair elections are conducted.

It is not clear, however, who the principal international community players would be and, more importantly, what their motivations and goals would be for a post-Castro Cuba. The "usual suspects" at the symbolic negotiating table will likely include some creditors from whom the Castro government and Cuba's state-owned enterprises have borrowed heavily. As of the end of 2008, Cuba's total known foreign debt in convertible (hard) currencies was nearly $32 billion, most of it in default. Of this sum, over 50 percent was owed to Castro's Cuba political allies such as Venezuela ($11.37 billion), China ($3.2 billion), post-Soviet Russia ($1.2 billion), Iran ($656 million), and Vietnam ($297 million). An additional Soviet-era debt to Russia is estimated at 20.848 billion in transferable rubles. Cuba's other billion-dollar creditors include Spain ($3.2 billion), Japan ($2.8 billion), Argentina ($2.0 billion), France ($1.9 billion), and Romania ($1.2 billion).[81]

Presumably, all of these countries will be looking to secure payment promises from a post-Castro government. However, notwithstanding the large debt considerations, or perhaps because of it, some of Castro's Cuban political allies may see it in their best interest to promote a regime of communist continuity rather than a transition to democracy and free markets. That is, the international community that will seek to influence events in post-Castro Cuba may include, among others,

---

81   "Cuba Hard Currency Debt, 2008." *Cuba Facts.* Issue 47. Cuba Transition Project, Institute for Cuban and Cuban-American Studies. May 2009.

the governments of Hugo Chavez, Vladimir Putin, and Mahmoud Ahmadinejad.

Lustration

General Douglas MacArthur, after his abrupt dismissal as Commander in Chief of the United Nations forces in Korea, recalled in his speech before a joint session of Congress an old barracks ballad which proclaimed, "Old soldiers never die; they just fade away." The Cuban generals will not just fade away, and hopefully they will keep their troops in the barracks. The first successors to Castroism will have to be nudged, or persuaded at the negotiation table, to conduct free and fair elections. Naturally, their first concern will be: What happens to us? Answering this question involves the first and most delicate series of decision making processes for successfully transitioning from fifty years of totalitarian rule to democratic governance.

In the period after the fall of the various European Communist States in 1989–1991, the term "lustration" came to refer to policies of limiting the participation of former communist government officials, especially informants of the communist secret police, in the successor governments or even in civil service positions. In modern times, lustration has taken the meaning "to purify" from the Latin historical sense, and it has been applied to the procedures a country undertakes to deal with past human rights abuses or injustices. Lustration laws will necessarily be part of any comprehensive reform process. The question "What happens to us?" is of paramount importance for Cuban officials in every corner of the massive and pervasive governmental bureaucracies, particularly for the higher level initial successors to Castroism that will sit at the negotiating table. Can they be expected to negotiate their demise? How can revanchist sentiments be addressed?

A panoramic overview of some of the approaches implemented by various Eastern European countries serves to illustrate the topic. To anchor the later Cuba discussion, the overview of generic approaches to lustration below follows closely the taxonomy and organizational scheme of Break, Gradualism, Pact, Reconciliation, Minimalism, and Continuity offered by Fredo Arias King, as his work in this field is particularly suited for present purposes. [82]

Break—In this approach, the new government prohibits the participation of high officials from the previous regime in the new government, as well as the participation of secret police collaborators in several of the new governmental institutions.

Gradualism—Gradual and ad hoc replacement of the principal functionaries of the previous regime without special lustration laws.

Pact—Gradual changes, also without special lustration laws, resulting from a transition pact with the previous regime,

Reconciliation—Changes take place within the framework of "reconciliation" and "cooperation" between the new and the previous political forces.

Minimalism—Minimal changes, given that the new leaders come from the old system.

Continuity—Insignificant changes, given also that all the new leaders come from the old system.

Each of the former Soviet Union countries handled its new relationship with the old totalitarian administration in its own way, and so will Cuba. Simplistically, they could be dichotomized into those that replaced the old leadership and those that did not. The taxonomy above offers a more nuanced classification. One pivotal argument was the necessity of retaining the old guard for reasons of reconciliation and governability. The previously noted experience of the United Sates in Iraq after disbanding Saddam's military and political apparatuses makes this point.

Central to a process of institutional de-communization, and intimately related to the big picture "lustration" question, is the narrower question of what to do with the files and personnel of the secret police and other repressive institutions and how to handle human rights abuses by their personnel. To a large extent, the approaches to lustration adopted derived from how the transition came about. If a transition pact had been negotiated, the new leaders were constrained

---

82 Arias King, Fredo. Op Cit.

as to how they could proceed in the personnel domain. In some cases, formal lustration laws were implemented prohibiting the participation of secret police officers and other high-level officials in sensitive positions in the new government for a specific period of time, e.g., five years. Secret police files were confiscated and placed under the control of newly created commissions often led by well-known opponents of the previous regime. In other cases, lustration laws were adopted prohibiting the participation of intelligence officers, but not necessarily that of Communist Party members.

Lustration laws were controversial and judged by some to be unjust and in violation of human rights. On the other hand, they tended to receive popular support, since they represented a clean break from the communist government and suggested a genuine transition. Lustration laws are either viewed as a witch hunt to some who advocate a "forgive and forget" approach in the interest of social harmony and reconciliation, or as a form of justice to others who argue that former communists will not be loyal to the new government. It was, and is, a legitimate debate as to what actions to take. In general, there was no systematic, comprehensive *de jure* lustration of all communist officials. Judicial procedures were instituted against only a relatively small group of individuals charged with criminal acts. It was argued, not without some merit, that in the end, all had been victims of the communist system. Grey areas abounded. There was, however, a healthy *de facto* lustration over time.

The controlling idea was not one of vengeance or punishment, but rather a determination to gain control of the official and unofficial governing mechanisms and levers of power of the former regime. This should also be the controlling idea in post-Castro Cuba, where the historical political culture embodies an unfortunate readiness to resort to violence in the pursuit of political aims. Indeed, some people must be dismissed and replaced, but the process can be structured not unlike what takes place in democratic countries with every change in administration. The struggle is not necessarily over ideology, but between those used to functioning under the rules of the old system and those looking to implement a constitutional system. *De facto* lustration can be approached strictly as a future-oriented bureaucratic and administrative function. Lustration can seek to separate functions between politicians and civil service employees. It can be accomplished via specific competency requirements and competition among candidates for a position. Meritocracy, transparency, and accountability can be effectively used to implement a "velvet" lustration. But there must be lustration if obstructionism is to be defeated.

The Cuban Lustration Dilemma

The Eastern European and the Russian experiences show convincingly that the end of communism does not necessarily mean the end of power and privilege for the ruling elite and nomenklatura. Negotiated transitions to democracy—as is likely to be the case in Cuba—will leave many of the former bureaucrats in control of the resources and institutions they had previously managed. Unfortunately, in Russia and elsewhere, the transition has been not from totalitarianism to democracy, but from communism to cronyism and systemic corruption, often involving the previously ruling elites.

In post-Castro Cuba, defeating obstructionism to legitimate reforms and avoiding widespread corruption will be a monumental task. Even reform-minded holdover government officials will have an obstructionist bias if they perceive little personal gain (by legitimate means) or large losses from profound reforms. At each reform decision point, they are likely to place a political Pascal's Wager. French philosopher Blaise Pascal offered that even though the existence of God cannot be determined through reason, a person should "wager" and act as if God exists. By doing so, the individual has everything to gain (Heaven if God does exist) and nothing to lose if He does not exist. Holdover Cuban government officials that embrace democratic changes will perceive "no personal gain," and perhaps even some losses, if democracy prevails. If democratic reforms fail and their former colleagues return to power, they will lose big for having supported the changes. Obstructing reforms may also be a "no personal gain" condition if democratic changes succeed, but obstructionism offers the opportunity to fight another day with their own platform if democratic reforms fail. In this decision making matrix under uncertainty, the Cuban nomenklatura's logical wager is to obstruct reforms. They have a vested interest in the preservation of the existing order or minimizing changes to it. From their point of view, an ersatz transition is their best bet for personal gain.

The legacy of the Castros regime and Cuba's historical path has left the country ill-prepared to undertake democratic reforms, but most importantly ill-prepared to sustain a democratic future. Moreover, any post-Castro regime will have plausible political arguments to delay, postpone, and manipulate genuine reforms both politically and economically. Just as importantly, the opposition in its fragmented, repressed, and penetrated state will be unable to launch an effective independent challenge for power.

The distressing reality is that Cuba today has no *in situ* democratic political class or alternative elite to replace the governing body. The lustration predicament is that in order to achieve a successful transition to democracy and a market economy, a clean, quick, decisive break with the communist past is required. And yet, necessarily, a negotiated transition of sorts must ensue with a post-Castro nomenklatura devoid of a democratic culture and predisposed to obstructionism.

Compounding the problem is the fact that the regime has systemically violated human rights abundantly, and a key lustration question centers on whether blame rests with the system or also with specific individuals, and where and how should those lines be drawn. The demand for justice is one of the basic ethical postulates of all humans. But dispensing timely justice where no impartial, independent, or competent judiciary exists is filled with existential perils for Cuba's democratic future. As in many other areas, the personnel dilemma in post-Castro Cuba will require difficult tradeoffs between justice and the rebuilding of the country and Salomonic decision making.

Transition scholars agree that no universal prescription exists to deal with the myriad issues involved in rebuilding a country along democratic lines. There are no specific, practical recommendations equally valid for all nations. But the change of systems is above all an autocatalytic political process. As such, the requirements of democracy must take priority and supremacy. Expanding the political contours is a necessary condition. In other words, a stable, prosperous Cuba cannot emerge from a transition regime based on single-party communist ideology or military-led authoritarianism.

As difficult as it may be for many Cubans to accept, the way out of this personnel transition quandary pivots on a willingness of all parties to leave mistakes in the past and focus instead on the salvation of the country's collective future. That is, on a collective willingness to support a political class untainted by venality and committed to liberal democracy regardless of their previous political affiliations or place of residence. To be clear and consistent with the main premise of this work, this is not about embracing venal economic reformers in the nomenklatura or elsewhere uncommitted to political reforms. The experience of the Soviet-bloc countries shows clearly how easily well-connected, self-serving, communist bureaucrats became eager "capitalists" overnight without a modicum of democratic inclination. The key personnel transition issue is to reverse the practice of capricious and arbitrary exercise of authority and construct the institutional framework for decision-making under the rule of law.

In order to avoid political stasis or chaos in post-Castro Cuba, a new way of perceiving the future and of behaving as a people must emerge. Conflicting political cultures, like scorpions in a bottle, cannot permanently avoid each other. But, political cultures, unlike scorpions, need not engage in an elimination fight to the end. They can coexist in a participatory democratic milieu provided that all participants accept democratic means as the field of engagement.

Carlos Alberto Montaner, discussing the Spanish Transition and its lessons for Cuba, notes that prior to the 1977 elections in Spain, Prime Minister Adolfo Suárez realized that "democracy could only be engendered in a collaborative initiative that included the communists as well as the socialists. As such, the *quid pro quo* came into focus: everybody could participate in a level playing field in exchange for institutional harmony."[83] Similarly, post-Castro Cuba must offer a

---

83 Montaner, Carlos Alberto. *The Spanish Transition and the Case of Cuba*. Miami. Institute for Cuban and Cuban-American Studies. 2002. http://ctp.iccas.

tolerant and enlightened *quid pro quo* of expanded political contours that includes subscribers of the current political model, but only those ready to accept the "absoluteness and finality of the law."

Earlier in this chapter the question "What happens to us?" was posed as being of paramount importance for Cuban officials in every corner of the massive and pervasive governmental bureaucracies, particularly for the higher-level initial successors to Castroism who will sit at the negotiating table. The answer is that they must perceive a lawful opportunity to participate in their country's future, provided they acknowledge and agree to the democratic process and elections as the main determinants of who will govern and for how long. Without such a collective change of strategic positioning and posturing, the Cuban nomenklatura and the opposition will find themselves in a sort of Nash equilibrium, where neither side has anything to gain by unilaterally changing strategies.[84]

---

miami.edu/research_studies/camontaner.pdf

84 In game theory, Nash equilibrium (named after John Forbes Nash, who proposed it) is a solution concept of a game involving two or more players in which each player is assumed to know the equilibrium strategies of the other players, and no player has anything to gain by changing only his or her own strategy unilaterally.

Chapter X – Institutional Reforms

Dejad que los perros ladren, es señal de que
vamos cabalgando.

Así le dijo el Quijote a Sancho Panza

THE DE-COMMUNIZATION OF CUBA FROM totalitarianism and a
command economy to a liberal democracy and its attendant market
economy requires the creation of many new institutions to support the
new polity and economic system. De-communization in the political
realm will require new institutions to reform the electoral system,
the structure of government, political parties, constitution writing,
prosecution of human rights abuses, restitution of past injustices, and
more.

In the economic realm, institutions and agencies will be required to
facilitate, oversee, and regulate the functioning of free and fair markets,
macroeconomic stabilization, liberalization of prices, privatization,
trade liberalization, taxation, and the like. In liberal democracies, the
individual serves as the foundational element for the organization of the
polity rather than a class, party, military establishment, or vanguard, as
in totalitarian regimes. Thus the de-communization process involves
a fundamentally different understanding of the structure and role of
institutions than the one familiar to Cubans.

Since the collapse of the Soviet Union, a vast academic, scholarly,
and practitioner's literature has emerged that examines in great detail
every aspect of the transitioning countries' experiences in implementing

reforms. Successes and failures have been carefully studied by "transitologists" of all disciplines, perhaps most of all with respect to economic reforms. Much can be learned from these works, but also, and perhaps more relevantly, from the works of hundreds of Cuban-American scholars of democratic and economic development. These professionals are immensely talented in their disciplines and intimately familiar with Cuba and its issues. The Institute for Cuban and Cuban-American Studies' Cuba Transition Project at the University of Miami and the Association for the Study of the Cuban Economy (ASCE) are just two such organizations that have published extensively on the many transition topics. The discussion in this chapter will focus more on how the implementation of institutional reforms must be guided by a fundamental supra-institutional principle: to resurrect Cuba's civil society from the corrosive effects of Castroism on the development of a democratic culture.

At the most basic level, institutions generate the informal social norms and the formal legal rules that govern individual behavior and structure interactions between individuals. Consequently, de-communization will require the expeditious and decisive disbanding and confiscation of the files and resources of the most toxic anti-democratic institutions of the old regime, particularly the Ministry of Interior (MININT) and the internal security apparatus, secret police, and related institutions used by the regime for internal coercive controls. Both of these sets of reforms, the creation of new institutions and the dismantling of the coercive control apparatus, must take place, and in fact the entire reform process must take place in an unprecedented environment of transparency.

The shared beliefs of legal cultures and practices, including respect and adherence to the rule of law, and to modern legal doctrines and values of constitutionalism are not inherent in Cuban contemporary culture and will have to be constantly fostered. A law-based state is not based solely on legal codes. It is based on the values and attitudes toward the law of the individuals that must obey the laws. The transition from communism will be a decisive founding event for Cuban society.

In communist societies, political conflict-resolution processes are officially discredited in favor of dogma. The mode and character of the transition will be an important factor in determining whether democracy will emerge and be sustained in post-Castro Cuba. Cubans will be more likely to feel psychologically invested in a legitimate transition if they see themselves as participants in the transition. Transparency and accountability are essential to involve the Cuban people, even if only vicariously as spectators, in the transition process. A corollary to this assertion is that the transitioning Cuban government cannot be a direct, ideological extension of the Castros' regime. Transition in post-Castro Cuba cannot become a mutation of Castroism. It needs to be its antithesis.

In this respect, the end-game for Cuban communism, regardless of how it comes about, will present an opportunity for the new leaders to implement a clean break with the past. When Castroism ends, the Cuban economy will be in deep crises and in total disarray. These objective conditions will constitute the Cuban collective memory of communism. Behavioral economists speak of the "peak-end rule," which states that we judge the past almost entirely on the basis of how the experience was at its peak and at its end. In other words, it is the positive or negative experiences at the end of a process that stay with us rather than some net average for the entire duration of the event. At the end of Castroism, Cuban society and economy will be in shambles and, at that time at least, any prior fondness for communist rule will be negated.

This "peak-end rule" condition offers the most important opportunity for quick and profound reforms enjoying overwhelming popular support. However, because reforms will take time to produce results, they will entail a degree of gratification delay. In essence, transitions offer a relatively short window of opportunity or honeymoon period. In this period, transition leaders will have to implement what behavioral scientists call "inter-temporal choices." That is, decisions that require tradeoffs among cost and benefits occurring at different times. Post-Castro Cuba will face many such inter-temporal choices in all sociopolitical and economic domains. Research shows that most people must be offered incentives in order to delay gratification and opt for long-term options. For economists, this is analogous to the principle that time discounts value, where value is a measure of the relative satisfaction gained from a transaction. The delayed gratification of inter-temporal policy choices must be somehow addressed by transition leaders.

Transparency and accountability in government activities are methods of offering the Cuban population psychological incentives to delay gratification. Transparency and accountability offer intrinsic value to a Cuban society unaccustomed to these values. They will help to increase the popular satisfaction gained from the transition transactions. For Cuban civil society the transition process must offer not vacuous statements or *status-quo* guided reforms, but a high degree of perceived value in the short, intermediate, and long-term. The psychology of turning former adversaries into a loyal opposition requires the creation of social institutions of perceived value that enable trust and reinforce positive social interactions. For the Cuban people, participation in the transition process via transparency and accountability in governmental decisions is a first and necessary condition to gain popular trust in the short-term. They, of course, must be accompanied and followed by results and excellence in governance in the longer term. The resurrection of Cuba's civil society is a prerequisite condition to sustain democracy. That resurrection begins with transparent and accountable governance.

As noted earlier, the principal objective of these reflections is not to offer detailed, step-by-step reform recommendations, but rather to offer reasoned first principles and trenchant observations that may serve one day as a compass to the new generation of leaders that will be responsible for bringing about changes in post-Castro Cuba. Transparency in all government activities is one such principle that unfortunately is often offered in platitudes and received superficially. But for Cuba's post-Castro transition, transparency will be essential if societal and institutional trust is to be rebuilt. For Cuba's future, transparency, as a first principle, is not a high-minded, abstract construct. It is perhaps the most readily available, powerful, and practical governance tool accessible to reformers to begin reversing the pernicious legacy of Castroism. Reformers need to apprehend and adopt transparency values equal to or surpassing those in place in developed countries. Transparency should not be viewed as a future idealistic goal or something to put in place after the transition. Transparency is a readily available practical instrument for good governance.

The intellectual and operational frameworks for transparency in governance are readily available in developed countries in the form of disclosure requirements of all kinds, sunshine laws, freedom of information acts, web sites, public hearings, and the like. These mechanisms can be easily adapted and promptly adopted by a transition government. A transition ruled by omnipresent transparency offers the best prospects to begin the process of trust-building required for the eventual emergence of a civil society. Transparency in governance is an antidote for the pervasive controls over and distortion of information that Cubans have experienced for over fifty years. It may very well come as a cultural shock of sorts to the population, but it will be a salutary, welcomed shock.

Trust in the new institutions or in the reformers themselves will not come about from political exhortations, grandiose speeches, or by government edict. Transparency is one of the few society-transforming government actions that can be implemented by fiat and at low cost to the country's treasury. It offers a feedback method—or a window into the workings of government—for the population to begin assessing and evaluating the transitional changes, the emerging institutions, and their new political leadership. It is a method that Cubans can use to begin participating, even if only intellectually, in the social and economic reconstruction of the nation.

Just as importantly, transparency requirements constitute the most effective deterrent to corruption and to poor management that a new transition government can implement in short order. Institution building takes time, particularly building independent law and order institutions. A most daunting phenomenon of transitioning countries and many (if not most) countries in the developing world is that an independent, honest, competent, judiciary has remained a goal rather than a reality. In most of the developing world, truly independent judges are still hard to find. Moreover, developing societal trust in those institutions is a very long-term endeavor. Pervasive transparency in government activities can, in some ways, fill the time voids and function as an imperfect substitute until law and order institutions can gain the respect of the population.

Transitions from authoritarianism to democracy are associated with large-scale increases in corruption and criminality. Transparency, raised exponentially when augmented with information technologies and with a vigorous free press, will serve to ameliorate the corruption patterns. Transparency, communications, and the constant surveillance of governmental affairs by an energetic free press offers post-Castro Cuba the first and best line of defense against corruption.

It is instructive to recall here that of the seventy-five members of the opposition imprisoned by the Cuban government during the infamous *Primavera Negra de Cuba* (the Black Cuban Spring) crackdown of 2003, twenty-seven were engaged in independent journalism. As Winston Churchill noted, "A free press is the unsleeping guardian of every other right that free men prize; it is the most dangerous foe of tyranny … the vigilant guardian of the rights of the ordinary citizen." It is for this reason that totalitarian governments view journalists as significant threats to power and so repress them. Independent journalists such as Yoani Sanchez and Claudia Cadelo will be invaluable during and after a transition, as they will help make the government's actions transparent for the Cuban people.

The theoretical construct here is to use transparency to reframe the transition process in an intimate short-term context immersing all Cubans in the transition program. The use of referendums is just one mechanism that may be employed to nudge a reluctant population to take a personal stake in the process. The dismally low turnout in the Eastern European June 2009 European Parliament elections illustrates how difficult it is to persuade voters that their institutions can do anything meaningful to solve their most immediate problems. The average turnout for the ten former communist countries was just over 31 percent, compared with an overall average of 43.1 percent for the twenty-seven-nation European Union. Although voters stayed away from the polls all across Europe, the trend was particularly surprising in the former communist countries, where a desire to participate in electoral processes could be expected to be higher after decades under communist rule, when the citizenry could not express itself in free elections.

Initially, trust is established through transparency. Later, it must be reinforced by the rule of law and by good governance and superb management of public affairs. In order for a post-Castro Cuba to transition successfully to democracy and free markets, society needs to develop both psychological-level trust and the social-level technologies (e.g., institutions) that reinforce trust. It is the psychology of trust that enables a society to advance and prosper. Transparency begins the building of psychological-level trust and aids the later development of institutional-level trust. The critically needed trust of institutions in Cuba will not occur until the citizenry tacitly agrees to obey the rules. And that, in turn, will not happen without transparency and trust.

Parenthetically, and we will return to this topic in the later discussion of economic reforms, trust is among the most powerful stimulants for investment and economic growth. The simple correlation between national rates of investment and trust is strongly positive. Simply put, when trust is low, investment lags. Research shows that trust is a very strong predictor of national prosperity. Consider for example a 1996 study on trust in forty-two countries where researches asked, "Generally speaking, would you say that most people can be trusted, or that you cannot be too careful in dealing with people?" In Brazil and Peru only 3 and 5 percent respectively reportedly believe that their fellow citizens are trustworthy. At the high end of the trust scale were Norwegians, with 65 percent, and Swedes, with 60 percent reporting trust in their fellow countrymen. The United States at 36 percent and the United Kingdom at 44 percent came in at the middle of the scale. The lowest trust levels were found in South America, Africa, and especially in the former communist bloc countries.[85] It is left for the reader to ponder where Cuba would rate in this trust scale.

---

85   Shermer, Michael. Kindle location 3507.

Fuerzas Armadas Revolucionarias: A Farewell to Arms?

In 1939, Winston Churchill famously described the Soviet Union as "a riddle wrapped in a mystery inside an enigma." The same can be said of the role that Cuba's Revolutionary Armed Forces (FAR) may play, initially and over time, in the various transition scenarios. Throughout the Castro era, the FAR has been the most powerful, influential, and professional institution in Cuba and, as noted in the preceding chapter, any conceivable negotiated transition process will necessarily involve military leaders. For all practical purposes, the FAR is the only game in town, controlling all coercive forces on the island, including the Ministry of Interior (MININT), which was placed under MINFAR's control in 1989. It is also Cuba's major economic player, controlling all key industries. By some estimates, FAR officers manage over 60 percent of the country's economic output.

Notwithstanding the FAR's predominance in Cuba's politico-economic life, its military capabilities have been seriously degraded, its command and control unity undermined, and its professionalism eroded. Contributing factors to the FAR's demoralization are the manifest corruption of senior officers involved in enterprise management, lingering tensions from the Ochoa affair of 1989, budget reductions, generational stresses, changing roles and missions, and more.[86] Independently of the role that the FAR plays in the early transition process, it will be a budgetary necessity for Cuba's political leaders to seriously and courageously rethink the country's military requirements as a democratic state in the twenty-first century. The economic question is straightforward. The allocation of Cuba's very limited economic resources needs to prioritize reconstruction efforts

---

86 The Ochoa Affair refers to the trial and execution of Gen. Ochoa and three others: FAR Capt. Jorge Martinez Valdes, MININT Col. Antonio de la Guardia, and MININT Maj. Amado Padron Trujillo. They were charged with drug trafficking, although it is well known that the reason behind their executions was politically motivated, with rumors of their impending defection or opposition to Fidel Castro. For more information, see Alonso, Jose F. "The Ochoa Affair and its Aftermath." In Irving Horowitz's *Cuban Communism*. New Jersey, Transaction Publishers. 1998.

and helping the population with basic needs. Post-Castro Cuba cannot afford large military expenditures. The social and political questions are more complex and daunting.

From the point of view of external military threats, the empirical case is also relatively straightforward. As an island country, Cuba has no land borders to defend. Cuba has no historical enemies in the hemisphere or elsewhere; certainly none interested in, or militarily capable of, launching a naval-based attack on the island. In short, a democratic Cuba faces no external danger of conventional military conflict. As noted by Brian Latell, a longtime Latin American specialist for the Central Intelligence Agency (CIA) who served as U.S. National Intelligence Officer for Latin America (1990–1994), "The three large regional armies are obsolete and unnecessary for Cuba's contemporary defense needs. They should be disbanded and perhaps replaced by air mobile regiments that could quickly be moved around the island if needed."[87]

There is also a wealth of empirical evidence showing the high positive correlation between liberal democracy and peace. Michael Shermer cites a number of studies in his book *The Mind of the Market*, particularly a study by political scientist Rudolf J. Rummel showing that 371 international wars occurred between 1816 and 2005 in which at least a thousand people were killed. Of these, 205 wars (55 percent) were between non-democratic nations. One hundred and sixty six wars were between democratic and non-democratic nations, and no wars took place between democratic nations.[88] Liberal democracies are very unlikely to wage war on each other.

Threats to a liberal democratic post-Castro Cuba requiring the use of military force are most likely to originate from internal sources and/or be linked to drug trafficking. One can hope that five decades of Castroism will have left the Cuban population exhausted of militaristic

87 Latell, Brian. *The Cuban Military and Transition Dynamics*. Miami. Cuba Transition Project. 2003. http://ctp.iccas.miami.edu/Research_Studies/BLatell.pdf

88 Rummel, Rudolf, J. *Power Kills: Democracy as a Method of Nonviolence*. New Brunswick. Transaction, 1997.

revolutionary inclinations. But Cubans have an unfortunate historical tradition of pursuing political goals by the force of arms. In the early post-Castro transition years, it is possible—perhaps even likely—that dissatisfied and marginalized elements of the communist regime will organize insurgencies. The same may occur in later years, if the transition turns antidemocratic, ineffective, or corrupt. Likewise, significant threats to the state may originate with homegrown or foreign illicit drug organizations. The island offers a strategic transshipment point for drugs entering the United States, as well as favorable conditions to become an important processing base. The FARC (*Fuerzas Armadas Revolucionarias de Colombia*) and the drug lords in Mexico and Afghanistan offer ample evidence of the social, political, and military firepower that drug-financed organizations can muster and the threats they represent. A post-Castro Cuba will be particularly vulnerable to increased organized criminality from both internal and external sources. This is the type of criminality that cannot be fought exclusively with the resources of civilian law and order organizations. Criminal enterprises financed by drug traffic display and use social, political, and military firepower, and will need to be fought in all three domains.

During his first term as president of Costa Rica (1948–1949), visionary leader José Figueres Ferrer boldly broke with Latin American patterns and abolished the country's army. This decision has helped the country elude the familiar Latin American traditions of war, poverty, and repression. Regrettably, the early post-Castro transition period in Cuba will not offer the propitious conditions to follow Pepe Figueres's example and bring about a farewell to arms. It will be, however, the time to reorganize Cuba's military capabilities to meet the new challenges Cuba will face as a young vulnerable democratic state. Generals are often criticized for being backward looking and always planning (or misplanning) to fight the last war rather than looking forward to emerging threats. In a democratic post-Castro Cuba, the successor to the FAR needs to be a force focused on a new role and mission of preparing to fight possible insurgencies and drug lords and not a U.S. invasion.

The particular military reconfiguration and tasking of such a force is best left to the military experts working under the leadership of a civilian defense minister in the democratic tradition. In principle, what may be needed is a sharply reduced voluntary, depoliticized force of four to six combat ready mobile brigades professionally trained and equipped as a counterinsurgency force, perhaps in a joint forces configuration. In the realm of wishful thinking, the day may indeed come when Cubans can say a definitive farewell to arms, but the post-Castro transition period will not offer that opportunity.

The Elusive "Government of Laws, and Not of Men"

John Adams's precept of "a government of laws, and not of men" —the idea that the law is above everyone and applies to everyone— will surely appear as a novel, abstract philosophical concept to most Cubans familiar only with the cult of personality fostered by Fidel Castro. The fact, of course, is that the rule of law is an ancient ideal that preoccupied the Greek philosophers and other thinkers. Establishing "a government of laws, and not of men" will be one of the most important and critical elements of the post-Castro transition. It will also be one of the most difficult. Even more daunting will be the task of engendering a "culture of law" in a population that disregards laws, viewing them as impediments to daily life and their *modus vivendi*. A law-based society can only flourish if citizens believe in the rule of law per se and are willing to subordinate their short-term interest to the supremacy of the law.

Consider a quotidian example: We are driving to work early in the morning to avoid the rush hour traffic and to get an early start on the day. At the stop sign intersection ahead, there are no other vehicles in sight, much less a police officer. And yet, subordinating our short-term interest of moving on, we dutifully come to a full stop (or maybe a rolling stop) as silently commanded by the impotent red sign. Consider the same situation in many developing countries, where traffic signals are routinely dismissed as mere "suggestions" or ornamental items. Ordinary and frivolous as this example may be, it serves to illustrate the culture of law prevalent in the United States contrasted to those in many developing countries.

Perhaps a more suggestive and thought-provoking example of how a "culture of law" interacts with a given civil society is offered by an experimental approach to traffic management currently in place in the Dutch towns of Drachten and Makkinga. In these communities, authorities have removed all traffic signs. With no speed signs, no stop signs, no yield signs, no signs of any kind, the expectation is that, if people are not being told how to drive, they will drive more courteously and carefully. The underlying theory of this approach, according to the project's designers, is that rules strip us of our ability to be considerate, and we lose our independent capacity for socially responsible behavior. The greater the number of rules, the more people's sense of personal responsibility is blunted. Philosophically, this approach shifts the emphasis away from the government taking the risk to the drivers assuming responsibility for their driving behavior. Reportedly, the approach is working. People drive slower, and there are fewer accidents in the towns compared to when the traffic signs were in place. It appears that the insertion of uncertainty, by removing the traffic directives, has nudged people to drive more responsibly.

Developing an authentic culture of law is bound to require a multigenerational time span. Establishing respect for the law in post-Castro Cuba will be an epic endeavor that will require much more than the formulation of laws. Developing a law-based state, however, is a required condition for the advancement and consolidation of democracy and economic prosperity. Near the center of this endeavor is an independent judiciary that can earn the trust and respect of the population. It is important to repeat that this goal of truly independent judges, prosecutors, and other members of the judicial system remains a goal rather than a reality in many developing democratic countries. Given the deplorable state of Cuba's civil society and its idiosyncratic characteristics discussed in earlier chapters, the prospect of developing a law culture in short order seems to be another one of Jorge Luis Borges' *causas perdidas* (lost causes).

Rule of law as a concept is based on two straightforward principles: 1) laws must replace the arbitrary use of power, and 2) all persons are equal before the law and subject to it. The rule of law applies to those governing as well as to those governed. As such, the rule of law is one of the key dimensions that determines the quality of governance of a country. These will be unfamiliar and perhaps exotic concepts to Cubans conditioned by five decades of capricious and arbitrary rule by the Castro brothers. Initially, at least, these concepts will be looked at askance. It is one thing to comprehend a concept intellectually and quite another to apprehend it behaviorally.

Democratic consolidation and successful economic reforms require independent judiciaries that effectively protect political and property rights. Political states based on the rule of law are necessary to keep markets and economic activities free and fair. In line with the central thesis of this book, economic reforms pursued in a political system lacking transparency and accountability is a formulation sure to produce corruption, collusion, and patronage. It should also be noted here that corruption, collusion, and patronage add enormous sociopolitical and economic costs to society and impede the effectiveness and efficiency of social transactions. Economists label these as "transactions costs." These corruptive transactions costs are costs that Cuba simply cannot afford.

Accountability—and the role that an independent judiciary plays in it—is indispensable for democratic consolidation and effective economic reform. Transparency was earlier discussed as a powerful mechanism that post-Castro Cuban leaders need to embrace to begin the process of trust building. At a societal level, trust is established through institutions that enforce the rules and ensure the fairness and justice of encounters and exchanges. Institutions serve to encourage cooperative and pro-social behavior. Institutions also help to foster what social scientists call "moral path dependency." The term suggests that moral systems and behavior become dependent on the rules of the relevant environment or become locked into the channels of moral patterns exhibited by others in the environment.[89] Objective observers of Cuba's civil society under communism will attest how that system locked the society into a channel of double morality and societal distrust.

---

89   Shermer, Michael. Kindle location 4180.

Transparent institutions are vehicles to change the moral dependency paths of Cuban civil society.

Transparency, however, is not a sufficient condition. Transparency must lead to accountability. In political science, accountability is usually understood as the act of informing about one's actions and answering and taking responsibility for them. Accountability by itself does not necessarily entail punishment. A free press, for example, can promote accountability when it is willing and able to report on government malfeasance. It can influence public opinion and, in that fashion, influence the behavior of government officials. But that accountability does not translate into punishment in the legal sense. Oversight institutions often do not have a mandate to impose punishment. A more comprehensive understanding of accountability adds "enforcement."[90] Without viable structures in place to create and enforce firm and fair rules, citizens become more self-centered. Oversight institutions without power to sanction are perceived as weak and inefficient. In the end, if a system does not provide punishment for demonstrated abuses of authority, there is no rule of law. Ironically, the self-centeredness that pervades Cuban civil society today is akin to the "war of all against all" (*bellum omnium contra omnes*) that concerned Hobbes, Marx, and Nietzsche; a psychological war of all against all.

One of the dangers of any transition is that leaders—perhaps with the best of intentions—may seek to purposely emasculate accountability institutions to facilitate and accelerate policy implementation. This is a path that will surely lead to corruption, collusion, and patronage. Let's recall that the custom of using government funds for political purposes is deeply entrenched in Cuban culture and was a salient feature of Spanish colonial rule and the post independence period. Post-Castro Cuban leaders must avoid this misstep and foster transparency and accountability, even if it means a slower, more deliberate transition pace.

The Eastern European experience shows that speed in reforms is important, even critical, and that speed has intrinsic value. But speed

---

90 Manzetti, Luigi. "Political Manipulations and Market Reforms Failures." *World Politics 55*. April 2003, pp. 315-60.

also comes at a cost. Transitions scholars are in general agreement that there is no convincing theory or model to estimate the optimum speed of transition. Creating a modern, liberal, democratic state of law entails enacting constitutional, civil, and penal codes. It requires laws that regulate business activity in a way compatible with free market activities. If "shock therapy" is a desirable approach to economic reforms, then it must work in tandem with judicial and accountability "shock therapies" designed to strengthen institutions of accountability such as the judiciary while making sure the institutions themselves are accountable. If these reforms are not visibly in place, Cubans will begin to wrongly view corruption, collusion, and patronage as intrinsic qualities of market reforms.

The constitution of judicial institutions will affect the prospects for economic reforms and democratic consolidation. Research shows that "new judicial institutions in emerging democracies are shaped primarily by the strategies of dominant political actors who attempt to maximize the congruence of the judiciary with their interests and its responsiveness to their priorities."[91] There is consensus among political scientists and practitioners that judicial independence is a necessary condition for the effective protection of political rights. In the Eastern European experience, however, the inception of new democratic institutions was often constrained by norms, attitudes, and structural conditions inherited from the communist regimes. It must be remembered that political institutions produce distributional benefits that make some actors better off and other actors worse off. "In periods of democratic transition and constitution drafting, political parties will have preferences over judicial institutions and policies that maximize the congruence of the judiciary with their interest and the responsiveness of judges to their priorities."[92]

A key task for Cuba's transition leaders will be to provide for the insulation of judges and the new judiciary from political coercion or patronage. Before post-Castro Cuban courts can become agents of

---

91 Magalhanes, Pedro C. "The Politics of Judicial Reform in Eastern Europe." *Comparative Politics*. October 1999, pp. 43–62.

92 Ibid., p. 47

expurgation and assume the responsibility of punishing past human right abuses, they will have to be the objects of expurgation, setting the stage for a series of political-judicial conflicts. These tasks cannot be formally completed during the initial transitional stage. Perhaps the best that can be expected is that the process proceeds with speed and democratic vitality, and is governed by transparency and accountability principles, so that Cubans can begin to apprehend that in fact the government is accountable to them. Perhaps some level of corruption is inevitable in any post-totalitarian transition. The rule of law may not prevent corruption. What is essential, however, is that corruption does not take place with impunity. The Cuban people will be watching.

Chapter XI– Political Reforms

We shall not grow wiser before
we learn that much that we have
done was very foolish.

Friedrich August von Hayek

UNDERLYING THE PREVIOUS CHAPTER'S DISCUSSION is the dictum that when checks and balances are not in place, corruption in many forms will thrive. This, in turn, will undermine democratic and economic reforms. Transparency and accountability were exalted as readily available, low-cost methods of nudging political leaders and civil society towards better governance. But political and economic rationality often diverge. It is then that the political system per se must provide a propitious environment for conflict resolution. Cuba's republican history begins with a curious, and perhaps emblematic, example of the propensity to access extra-constitutional means in the name of good governance.

By most accounts, Tomás Estrada Palma, Cuba's first president, was an honest man who governed judiciously, guarding public expenditures and producing an impressive budgetary surplus during his first administration. But he did not hesitate to engage in electoral fraud in order to be reelected, fearing perhaps that his opponent, General José Miguel Gómez, would misuse the budgetary surplus Estrada Palma had so prudently produced. For Estrada Palma, and for practically all Cuban politicians since, the preferred modes of conflict resolution have not followed democratic patterns. Political reforms in post-Castro Cuba must take into account, and aim for, built-in mechanisms that will nudge all of society towards political strategies and choices for conflict resolution rather than violent undemocratic behavior. A good starting point for this discussion, therefore, is the modes of conflict resolution that will be needed for post-Castro Cuba to transition effectively and peacefully from totalitarianism to pluralistic democratic rule.

A transition from totalitarianism to democracy cannot be imposed; it must emerge from explicit and implicit bargaining among the various constituencies. The absence or failure of such bargaining efforts will obstruct progress toward the renaissance and consolidation of democratic values and a pluralistic political system. Political science professor Helga A. Welsh in her study of "Political Transition Processes in Central and Eastern Europe" notes:

> The successful transition process toward democratic political rule involves three stages. First, liberalization of the authoritarian regime is accompanied by declines in use of command and imposition as the prevailing modes of conflict resolution. Second, as the transition proceeds to extrication from the old regime and institutionalization of the new political system, bargaining and compromise emerge as the key features in decision making. Finally, consolidation of the transition is distinguished by the increasing dominance of competition and cooperation as the prevailing means of conflict resolution."[93]

In this context, transition scholars make the critical distinction between liberalization and democratization. Post-Castro Cuba may initially offer only an opportunity for liberalization, but not a move toward democratization. Extrication from totalitarian rule does not guarantee that the constitution of a democratic state will necessarily

---

93　Welsh, Helga A. "Political Transition Processes in Central and Eastern Europe." *Comparative Politics*. July 1994, pp. 379–394. Emphasis added.

follow. The collapse of totalitarianism in Cuba may result in a variety of outcomes, including a military dictatorship.

> First, transition periods are characterized by the need to address certain crucial issues under rather urgent time constraints ... Second, transition periods are characterized by great uncertainty with regard to both the process and the results ... Third, previous authoritarian structures are altered during a transition period by the rapidly expanding range of actors ... Fourth, transitions are elite-centered. Last, but not least, transitions involve bargaining."[94]

The critical point for current purposes is that whereas a "one-step" transition to democracy in post-Castro Cuba may be the most intellectually satisfying approach, it is unlikely that the transition will proceed from conflict resolution that is based on command and imposition to competition and cooperation, skipping the intermediate step of conflict resolution based on bargaining and compromise. Political and economic necessities will require bargaining and compromise, perhaps in the form of governments of "national unity" or "national responsibility," until pluralistic democratic elections can be held.

An important intellectual caveat is called for here regarding bargaining and compromise as intuitively understood and employed in democratic societies and in authoritarian regimes. For example, more often than not, the formulation of foreign policy in the United States and other democratic societies places a great deal of emphasis on goodwill negotiations based on principles of bargaining and compromise. This willingness to negotiate and compromise is what comes naturally in pluralistic political systems where competition is grounded in political climates that nurture compromise and cooperation. In contrast, bargaining and compromise in totalitarian regimes is initiated and controlled by the state and seeks primarily the protection and continuation of power.

---

94 Ibid., p. 382

Thus, in post-Castro Cuba, bargaining and compromise will be approached with fundamentally different mindsets by elements of the regime and by the opposition. Extrapolating bargaining and compromise as understood in pluralistic societies to its application in authoritarian settings fails to recognize that intellectually and culturally the very *raison d'être* for negotiating differs between the two systems. Bluntly stated, negotiations do not always work across political cultures.

These observations do not imply, however, that a slow gradualist approach to reforms is inevitable or desirable. In fact, keeping in mind the earlier discussion of the "peak-end rule," the considerations can now turn to "prospect theory"—a psychological theory of decision making under risk that suggests that the Cuban interregnum could support bold and risky policy choices.

Prospect Theory and the Prospects for Reform.

Prospect theory describes decisions between alternatives that involve risk; [95] that is, alternatives with uncertain outcomes as would be the case in post-Castro Cuba. As a descriptive model, it seeks to model real-life choices rather than optimal decisions. Politics is often described as dealing in the realm of the possible, thus prospect theory fits well with the uncertainty of transitions scenarios. An important implication of prospect theory—often used in behavioral economics— is that the way outcomes (or transactions) are subjectively framed in the minds of participants affects the utility they expect from the outcome. A related implication is that people consider not only their own utility value, but the utility received by others as well. That is, utility may be reference-based. These concepts are consistent with the psychological research into happiness discussed in Chapter VIII. A core finding of prospect theory is that people tend toward bold, risky choices when facing prospects of losses, but opt for caution when anticipating gains.

---

95 Prospect theory was developed in 1979 by Daniel Kahneman, of Princeton University's Department of Psychology and by Amos Tversky.

For current purposes, the fundamental implication is that leaders will enact, and citizens will support, drastic, rapid reforms when faced with profound social and/or politico-economic crises.

Kurt Weyland, professor of politics and government, has used prospect theory in his study "The Political Fate of Market Reform in Latin America, Africa, and Eastern Europe," which provides insights into the motivations of leaders to enact, and citizens to accept, drastic economic reforms despite the short-run costs.[96] Unquestionably, a genuine transition in post-Castro Cuba will require comprehensive shifts in attitudes in both the psychological and sociological domains to dislodge the status quo bias as the preferred point of reference. Both the leadership and the citizenship must shift from risk-aversion to risk acceptance. In bargaining and compromise, as well as in policy choices, a shift in attitudes must take place from resistance against temporary losses—as is the case in totalitarian regimes—to accepting the temporary losses that often accompany inter-temporal decisions. Implementing political and particularly economic reforms at a rapid pace can trigger social unrest. The question then becomes, what would make cautious and recalcitrant politicians and government officials embrace a bold program of reforms? More to the point, can they be nudged to undertake such reforms?

Prospect theory accounts for shifts in our propensities toward risk. "The central empirical finding of prospect theory is that people tend toward risky behavior when confronted with threats to their wellbeing, but are cautious when facing more auspicious prospects. Crises trigger bold actions, while better times induce risk aversion."[97] Working against this shifting propensity toward bold action is the status quo bias of entrenched bureaucrats. This status quo bias persuades long-standing political leaders, such as the Cuban nomenklatura, to stay on a failed path even though it may offer no chance of improvement. As Wayland points out, "Due to loss aversion and a reluctance to admit failure, people tend to persist in an uncompromising course of action,

---

96　Weyland, Kurt. "The Political Fate of Market Reform in Latin America, Africa, and Eastern Europe." *International Studies Quarterly*. 1998, 42, pp. 645–674.

97　Ibid., p. 648

hoping against all odds that it will finally bring success and thus erase past losses. … The status quo bias can thus keep in check the risk acceptance predicted by prospect theory. **Only new leaders** escape from this trap of sunk costs and respond to a deep economic crisis with drastic adjustment measures that repudiate established policies."[98]

Applying these insights of prospect theory to the politics of economic reforms, professor Weyland hypothesizes that new leaders, not subject to the status quo bias, respond to economic crises in risk-acceptant ways by choosing bold, drastic adjustment plans. On the other hand, long-standing leaders, subject to the status quo bias, avoid risky policy choices even when facing severe and deteriorating economic conditions. This, of course, has been the case under Castroism, where the geriatric leadership has failed to implement bold and comprehensive market-oriented reforms. A partial answer to the question presented above is that deplorable economic conditions alone will not persuade long-standing politicians and government officials to embrace a bold program of reforms. Wayland's work shows that countries adopt profound, comprehensive reforms when two conditions are met: 1) a deep economic crisis exists, and 2) new leaders ascend to power. These are also the conditions under which dramatic reforms would become politically viable in Cuba with the support, at least initially, of the citizenship. Thus, the depth and pervasiveness of the economic crises produced by Castroism, and its "peak-end rule" relevance in the collective memory of the population suggest—in line with prospect theory—that *only a new leadership would undertake the necessary reforms.* These notional insights of prospect theory were intuitively and accomplishedly understood by Václav Havel when he chose temporary inexperience over permanent sabotage (see Chapter VIII discussion).

---

98 Ibid., p. 649. Emphasis added.

The Bargaining and Compromise Stage

The discussion above has presented a number of conflicting points. Let's single out a few: Transition periods are characterized by the need to address many crucial issues under urgent time constraints. Yet, the status quo bias of long-standing government officials conspires against bold action. Transition periods are characterized by great uncertainties, as structures are altered by the rapidly expanding range of actors. Thus loss aversion and a reluctance to admit failure will work to obstruct reforms. Transitions are elite-centered and involve bargaining, but bargaining and compromise have different meanings and end-game objectives for the new and old elites. Thus, if post-Castro Cuba is unlikely to experience a one-step transition to democracy based on the immediate competition and cooperation of political parties, what then should be on the table during the intermediate bargaining and compromise stage until pluralistic democratic elections can be held?

The bargaining and compromise stage may indeed take a variety of forms and contexts depending on the political environment. The essential point, however, is that this stage be confined largely to the political realm. That is, to the dissolution of the totalitarian regime and to the procedures for the establishment of a pluralistic democratic government that gains legitimacy through free, fair, and competitive elections. The bargaining and compromise stage should have as its main—almost singular—goal the setting of terms for the creation of a new political system. This stage is not the time to negotiate economic reforms with an entrenched elite subject to the status quo bias and psychologically (and perhaps even intellectually) unable to undertake or support the bold economic reforms necessary for the country's economic recovery.

The opening paragraph of this book contrasts existentially two opposed systems of values: one in which primacy goes to human rights, freedoms, and democracy; and one in which priority is given to financial prosperity and economic growth. That argument is reformulated here in its most practical application, fully supported by our understanding of the status quo bias, prospect theory, risk aversion, and related topics. Bargaining and compromise with Cuba's long-standing elite, who do not target democratization, will not advance honest financial prosperity and economic growth. It will retard it. Undemocratic power sharing with a status quo-biased elite that has not been legitimized by free, fair, and competitive elections and subject to transparency and accountability will not facilitate the rapid transition from a centralized to a market economy. Just as importantly, it will not contribute to the resurrection of Cuba's civil society.

All transitions require bargaining and compromise. As a mode of conflict resolution, bargaining and compromise are preferable to the command and imposition mode of totalitarian regimes, but fall short of the competition and cooperation prevalent in pluralistic societies. For the first phase of post-Castro transition, elite bargaining and compromise will be the necessary modes of conflict resolution. But what must be on the negotiating table in this phase is not economic reform, but the dissolution of the totalitarian regime and the procedures for the establishment of a pluralistic democratic government. Why would the Cuban nomenklatura or the FAR agree to such an agenda? There are always the appeals to gallant, self-sacrificing patriotism and the national well-being, but let's keep the naiveté to a minimum and search for more realistic nudges.

Realistically, nudging the Cuban nomenklatura or the FAR out of their status quo bias and loss aversion defensive mechanisms will require that they perceive their future under a new democratic regime to be more comprehensively promising than their life prospects under a continuity regime. This, in turn, requires that they not be unjustly denied the opportunity to compete in the political processes and economic opportunities of post-Castro Cuba. There will be opportunities where they will, in fact, enjoy significant advantages.

In seeking to nudge the post-Castro Cuban leadership, it is essential to keep in mind some important implications of "prospect theory" noted earlier. The way outcomes (or transactions) are subjectively framed in the minds of participants affects their expected utility from the outcome, and people consider not only their own utility value, but the utility received by others as well. In this context of nudging the Cuban nomenklatura or the FAR out of their status quo bias and loss aversion mechanisms and into a democratic platform, Cuba's future, as well as their own, needs to be re-postulated as an ongoing struggle for personal freedoms. Freedom is perhaps the only philosophical concept capable of bridging the vast differences in sociopolitical and economic values and ideologies that exist in the Cuban nation. Notwithstanding the perks the nomenklatura may enjoy under a totalitarian regime, it is unlikely that they feel truly free. The opportunities for personal freedom can be a most powerful nudge.

The Early Elections Paradox

The free formation of political movements and parties of all kinds and ideologies is a feature of all post-authoritarian transitions. This is an important phenomenon that expresses the very essence of such transitions. It expresses the pent-up demand for political participation and the desire to be heard. But the proliferation of political groups presents challenges to the formation of an efficient government. In Poland by 1991, there were more than one hundred political parties competing for personal and political power. Lech Walesa humorously captured the situation by commenting, "When two Poles get together, three political parties emerge." That proportional rule is bound to be about the same for Cubans. In post-Castro Cuba, a proliferation of political groups, mostly brandishing slogans rather than substantive politico-economic programs, will contribute to the political confusion and fragmentation of the transition.

However, as discussed by James Madison in "Federalist Number 10," "The latent causes of faction are thus sown in the nature of man ... The regulation of these various and interfering interests forms the principal task of modern legislation, and involves the spirit of party and faction in the necessary and ordinary operations of the government."[99] Madison understood that the causes of fragmentation cannot be eliminated, and that restraining liberty to limit factions is an unacceptable solution.

---

99 Madison, James. "The Federalist No.10." *Daily Advertiser.* November 1787. http://www.constitution.org/fed/federa10.htm

In his thinking, factions were helpful in guarding against the cabals of a few. "Extend the sphere, and you take in a greater variety of parties and interests; you make it less probable that a majority of the whole will have a common motive to invade the rights of other citizens." For *mañana* in Cuba, the governing challenge will be to harness political diversity in a way that preserves freedoms and contributes to good governance.

As noted above, in this turbulent and uncertain post-Castro, pre-elections stage, bargaining and compromise will have to be the principal mode of conflict resolution. Some political contradictions will be at play that will need to be worked out. First, in order for the bargaining and compromise to have any chance of successfully moving on to a legitimate transition, the status quo biased elite (i.e., the communist regime's holdovers) must be offered an opportunity to compete. Without this inducement, the process cannot move peacefully to conflict resolution based on competition and cooperation. Second, the prompt scheduling of free, fair, inclusive, and competitive elections is necessary to legitimize the new government in the reform process. But the scheduling of early elections means that the reform forces will have little time to organize and compete with a long-standing elite (the Communist Party or its successor) that enjoys intrinsic organizational, financial, and institutional advantages.

Most importantly, however, will be the decisions over how the state's executive, legislative, and judicial organs are organized; that is, the decisions regarding the type of government best suited for post-Castro Cuba. Historically, Latin American countries influenced by the presidential system of the United States have, almost without exception, adopted presidential governing systems. In contrast, most of the new democracies in Central and Eastern Europe have opted for parliamentary or hybrid systems in their post-communism transitions.

More often than not, it is taken for granted that post-Castro Cuba should return to its pre-Castro constitutional arrangements (the 1940 Constitution) and its presidential system. However, that document, often nostalgically revered by Cubans of its generation, is an outdated, interventionist, over-specific, near-chauvinistic constitution unsuited for a twenty-first century liberal democratic state. It is also interesting to note—as Orlando Gutiérrez-Boronat does in "Cuba: A Nation in Search of a State" —how the language of successive Cuban constitutions and constitutional laws became increasingly state-centric, culminating in the replacement of the sovereignty of the people with the sovereignty of the state.[100]

The first article of the 1901 Constitution emphasized the people. It read that "the people of Cuba constitute themselves into an independent and sovereign state and adopt a republican form of government." The Constitutional Law of 1934 stated that "the people of Cuba are an independent and sovereign state, whose form of government is republican." The 1940 Constitution morphed into, "Cuba is an independent and sovereign state, organized as a unitary and democratic republic, for the attainment of political freedom, social justice, human solidarity, and individual and collective well-being." Finally, the 1976 Socialist Constitution epitomizes the state-centric nature: "the republic of Cuba is a socialist state of workers and farmers ..."

Moreover, the presidential system of government was not particularly successful in pre-Castro Cuba, and has, at best, a mixed record in Latin America. This is not to argue the relative merits and problems of presidential and parliamentary systems of governments. That subject is an ongoing polemic among political scientists that has endured generations of debate, and it is not about to be settled here. In any case, the concern here is not with the relative merits of the alternative systems of democratic governance in the abstract. This discussion is framed and limited by specific time and place considerations. What system of government may be best suited for post-Castro Cuba?

To be more specific, what system of government is best suited to the Cuban character, and to the social, political, and economic conditions that will prevail in the country after more than five decades of communist rule? Even more to the point, given the state of Cuba's civil society and the legacy of Castroism, does a parliamentary system of sorts offer better nudging mechanisms to guide Cubans in the direction of better governance? A brief and targeted overview of the

---

100 Gutiérrez-Boronat, Orlando. op. cit., p.50

basic typology of democratic governing systems will help here to consider what may work best *mañana* in Cuba.

Parliamentary versus Presidential Governments

In practice, every country that uses a presidential, parliamentary, or hybrid system to define the relationship among its governing institutions has its own variance of the selected system. Cuba, too, must adopt a system according to its particular needs. The individual characteristics of parliamentary, presidential, and hybrid systems are well known and do not need to be discussed here. For our discussion, it is only necessary to consider superficially three key aspects of the prototypical systems as they may be relevant to post-Castro Cuba: separation of powers, removal from office, and the structure of legislative parties and the leadership.

Presidential political systems, where the president is both the chief executive and the head of government, are characterized by a separation of powers, where the executive, legislative, and judicial branches of the government are independent of each other. This separation of powers is essential to protect citizens' rights, to prevent the abuse of executive powers, and for good governance in general. Without an effective separation of powers, all of these are at risk. One problem in this sphere is that most developing countries that have adopted presidential systems have failed to achieve truly independent judiciaries and an effective separation of powers even decades after the inception of the presidential system. Effective checks and balances are therefore compromised.

The probability that post-Castro Cuba will be somehow able to achieve a genuine separation of powers within a generation under a presidential system is close to zero. The longer-term prospects are not much better given the negligible progress in this area observable in the developing world. Under a presidential system, effective checks and balances will be missing in the Cuba of tomorrow. This is an unfortunate reality, but it is one that would be true by definition.

In a presidential system, in line with the notion of the separation of powers, the president and the members of the legislature are elected separately for a predetermined length of time. Arguably, this fixed term in office offers less timely accountability than systems where the term in office is more directly related to executive performance or parliamentary confidence in the executive. Finally, party discipline—defined as the practice of the legislature voting with their parties—is weaker in presidential systems.

Presidential systems have many desirable features, but the essential point for this discussion is that they rely on, and require, an authentic separation of powers for checks and balances to work adequately. This authentic separation of powers, in turn, requires a qualified, professional, independent judiciary—something that would require generations to flourish in post-Castro Cuba. In addition, the fix-term feature of presidential systems does not provide the sort of timely, performance-based accountability that will be so necessary to persuade the Cuban people that the government does, in fact, work for them and is accountable to them.

Parliamentary systems can be similarly criticized on many fronts, but these systems may offer the Cuba of tomorrow some "choice architecture" ways of achieving the good governance that has eluded the country for most of its history. In parliamentary governments, there is typically a clear differentiation between the head of state and the head of government. Often, but not necessarily, the head of state functions primarily in a ceremonial role. Also, unlike presidential systems, parliamentary systems are characterized by a fusion of powers between the legislative and executive branches.

A most striking difference between the presidential and parliamentary systems is that the chief executive in parliamentary systems is not chosen by the people but by the legislature. Parliament is sovereign and the executive authority that is exercised by the prime minister and his cabinet is derived from the legislature. This fusion of the legislative and executive branches in parliamentary governments leads to more discipline among political party members. Additionally, given the executive branch's association with the legislative branch, the head of government can be made more accountable for the executive branch's performance. Since a prime minister can serve only with the support of parliament—more specifically, with the support of his party in parliament—it becomes significantly easier to enact legislation into law. Party loyalty is critical for successful governance in a parliamentary system. The prime minister's government proposes legislation for parliament to vote on. In this respect, a prime minister enjoys legislative advantages that presidents might not. On the other hand, in the early post-Castro years, lack of party tradition, party identification, and programs, plus the mushrooming of political parties and more, may hinder efficient decision-making that is only possible with the support of a majority in parliament.

In parliamentary governments, the timely accountability of the prime minister is promoted by the mechanism for his removal. In these systems, the prime minister can be removed at any time through a successful "vote of no confidence," usually a motion introduced by the opposition or a coalition of opposition parties. The prime minister can also be removed by his own party members if the party decides to change its leader. The political history of Cuba from the beginning of the republic in 1902 to the Castro era suggests a penchant of Cubans to want to change leaders prior to the end of their constitutional terms. A parliamentary type of government may better accommodate this Cuban proclivity, particularly in the confusing and turbulent post-Castro years. This is not to suggest that frequent changes in government are desirable. What is desirable, however, is that they take place in accordance with the law and not by extra-constitutional means. Parliamentary systems provide constitutional options to address popular impatience and hold leaders accountable on the people's time table rather than on a fixed term in office. What this represents, with all its positive and negative implications for governance, is that the rule of law, and not *golpes de estado*, becomes the model for changing governments.

The first objection is that Cubans have absolutely no experience with parliamentary systems of government. But then again, after a century of mostly totalitarian and illegitimate governments, whatever collective memory remains of legitimate democratic presidential rule is, at best, nebulous and distant. In the end, the Cuban citizenry, as it struggles to identify itself as a post-Castro society, needs to adopt the form of democracy best suited for the new Cuba and not thoughtlessly retrace its past. This struggle for a new political identity may include both, a desire for a clean break with the past and also a certain level of the peculiar, but ever-present, Latin American form of anti-United States sentiment. Both can be addressed by adopting a parliamentary type of government.

In the economic discussion that follows in the next chapter, some arguments will be presented noting the necessity of integrating Cuba's economy with world markets, and in particular with the United States' market. In the economic realm, post-Castro Cuba will be heavily impacted by policies of the government of the United States, by American tourists, by the investments of American enterprises, by the Cuban-American community, and by all things American. A parliamentary system of government offers post-Castro Cuba a psychological opportunity, if one is needed, to establish a new political identity different from that of the United States. By adopting a parliamentary system, Cubans can establish their de rigueur credentials of independence and move quickly to develop strong economic ties with the United Sates.

In the political realm, specifically with respect to the system of government, Cuban leaders will be well advised to seek the guidance and counsel of the Eastern European countries that have most successfully extricated themselves from their communist past. Leaders such as Václav Havel, Lech Walesa, Václac Klaus, Mart Laar, and many others can offer Cuban leaders invaluable practical guidance into how one goes about building a democratic, market-oriented state. They understand the issues; they lived through both the problems of communism and the problems of transitioning. Understandably, at the beginning of the twentieth century, republican Cuba modeled its presidential system on the American original. By the middle of that century, Communist Cuba was using the Soviet model. Those copies did not fit the Cuban framework. Cuba's historical trajectory, as it emerges from communist rule in the twenty-first century, suggests that it should seek new inspiration in the experiences of the Eastern European nations that have experienced a similar trajectory in the recent past. One possibility is that Cuban leaders may seek to adopt a hybrid system of governance that blends features of the presidential and parliamentary systems.

A "Made In and For Cuba" Democratic Political System

Hybrid systems are those in which both a president and a prime minister are somehow relevant political players in the day-to-day administration of the state. A hybrid system differs from a classic parliamentary system in that it has a popularly elected head of state who is more than a ceremonial figurehead. Hybrid systems are termed semi-presidential systems if the president is constitutionally or conventionally empowered to select the prime minister. They are termed semi-parliamentary systems if the emphasis is on the power of the prime minister and parliament. In the French semi-presidential system, for example, the popularly elected president nominates the prime minister and selects his own cabinet. However, the day-to-day running of the government is left to the prime minister and cabinet, while the president may have other well-defined powers, such as the conduct of foreign affairs. Unlike classic parliamentary systems, the legislature cannot force the resignation of the popularly elected president. But, similarly to parliamentary systems, the legislature can force the prime minister to resign by passing a motion of censure. In the French model, the prime minister is accountable to and vulnerable to removal from both the legislature and the president under certain conditions.

It must be noted that hybrid systems are not a panacea; constitutional or political battles may develop over the relative rights and powers of the head of state and the head of government. Hybrid systems, particularly of the semi-presidential variety, can veer off the democratic track, as has been the case in Russia. Also, hybrid systems sometimes produce an uncomfortable condition of "cohabitation," where leaders from different parties must find ways to work together or face policymaking deadlock. But in the context of post-Castro Cuban politics, cohabitation may not be a totally undesirable condition. It may work as a nudge to move political leaders from conflict resolution modes based on command and imposition to bargaining and compromise. If that fails, and the government is dissolved, then the systems must rely on competition and cooperation for the election of a new parliament.

Awkward and paralyzing as these political processes may be, if they take place in full view of the population, they will serve as object lessons in democratic governance, an open classroom for the citizenry. Better yet, these political processes can be engaging daytime soap operas (*telenovelas*), with villains and heroes, for all Cubans to see and follow. Visible conflict resolution in governance based on bargaining, compromise, competition, and cooperation can begin the process of growing a civil society critical mass, one that, for the first time in Cuban history, will see the country's democratic institutions as truly their servants.

If a citizenry does not feel that a system belongs to them, if democracy becomes a political abstraction without real day-to-day context for the people, it is much more difficult to engage civil society. Democratic governance should become for Cubans a living, personal experience in which they are willingly engaged. Parliamentary or hybrid systems appear preferable to create a more natural and engaging organic bond between the citizenry and the government than presidential systems that touch the citizenry only tangentially every so often. The objective is to create greater coherence between Cuban society and its form of government. Democratic education begins with the reeducation of the ruling elite. In particular, it must begin with the notion that they are public servants and not enlightened messianic emissaries. Thus the fundamental question of governance for post-Castro Cuba is to identify and adopt a system that reconciles and integrates the citizenry with the system; a system that nudges the Cuban people to assume democratic responsibility for their own governance.

Cuban intellectual Carlos Alberto Montaner, an incisive observer of contemporary Latin American politics, has offered a hybrid system of the semi-parliamentary variety. In his version, a clear distinction is made between the government and the state. The head of the state—a president elected by popular vote—would function as ombudsman or chief defender of the people and whip for the bureaucracy. Montaner's version leaves the appointment of the prime minister with parliament and the day-to-day government administration in the hands of the prime minister. Montaner's design is more than an abstract intellectual construct. It offers the possibility to create an additional direct, practical connection between society at large and the government via the head of state. He seeks to create in the president a "social power" capable of advocating for the citizenry and strengthening the people's trust in the system. The idea needs to be elaborated to flesh out, and better delineate the respective powers of the head of state and head of government. But in principle, it offers the basis for a system-wide design of government that incorporates powerful nudges to incline both society and government in the direction of better and more accountable governance. For the Cuban people, the end of Castroism must bring about the integration of the relative weight of civil society with government in a way that is palpable and real via a democratic system of government made by Cubans and for Cubans.

Chapter XII – Economic Reforms

Those who cannot remember the past are condemned to repeat it.

George Santayana

THE DISCONNECTED DISCUSSIONS IN THE preceding chapters of personnel, institutional, and political reforms may create the impression that these reforms are somehow only tangentially related to each other. The fact is that they are intricately interconnected and interdependent. Post-Castro Cuba will have to undertake the simultaneous or near-simultaneous liberalization of its political and economic systems. The synthesis of Cuba's economic problems is that its centrally planned command economy and its totalitarian regime are not reformable and thus cannot serve as the starting point for the country's redevelopment. Therefore, before jumping right into the economic reform process, it is important to explore, if only briefly, how political and economic liberalization interact.

Cuba's post-Castro transition will come about after a prolonged period of economic decay. The initial conditions existing at the inception of the transition will be those of extreme impoverishment, which will require reformers to consider and account for myriad social factors when formulating economic policy decisions. The approach to these socioeconomic conditions cannot be predicated exclusively on the principles of technical economics but more inclusively on the spheres of political policymaking and political economics. A comprehensive reform program will demand political skills and statesmanship to a greater degree than technical economic proficiency.

Central to any approach to political and economic liberalization is the inescapable reality that policy measures will impose immediate and certain costs that are often concentrated on specific societal groups. In contrast, the benefits of reform measures to liberalize the economy tend to be more uncertain and diffused and not immediately apparent in the day-to-day lives of the citizenry. Often, the losing societal groups represent organized and powerful vested interests like the military establishment or the nomenklatura. Given that the gains for society at large are less certain and much more diffused, the potential winners are likely to be unorganized, resulting in an asymmetry of political influence between winners and losers. The unadorned reality is that programs of economic and political liberalization complement each other but will also be in conflict with each other.

Post-Castro Cuba cannot afford to postpone economic reforms, or to dilute them for political expediency, or to promote a politically calm atmosphere. The question of the speed of reforms is a controversial one. However, "there is a mass of historical and statistical evidence showing that the countries that take an early start in implementing substantial reforms perform better after a few years than the slower and more timid reformers."[101] The daunting task will be to undertake political and economic liberalization concerted in rapid sequencing which begs the question of what is the most propitious and constructive politico-economic sequencing. In this context it is helpful to keep in mind that when introducing reforms, the best can often be the enemy of the good. Problems cannot always be "solved," and trade-offs will need to be made.

In the 1970s and 1980s, some political theorists and political groups subscribed to the erroneous idea that authoritarian governments were particularly capable of, and perhaps even necessary to, implementing comprehensive and rapid market reforms. "Later studies largely discredited that simple assumption and stressed instead more sharply

---

101 Hernández-Catá, Ernesto. *Institutions to Accompany the Market in Cuba's Future Economic Tranistion.* Miami. Cuba Transition Project. 2005, p. 5.

specified state-centered variables such as electoral cycles and institutional arrangements, which give key economic officials substantial authority while insulating them from direct political pressures."[102] The topic, of course, pivots on what aspects of economic policymaking can be legitimately insulated from political considerations in a democratic system without stepping onto the perilous, slippery slope toward authoritarianism.

In the case of post-Castro Cuba, the five-plus decades of economic decline and mismanagement brought about by collectivism will have convinced much of the population of the need to implement difficult and painful reforms. In fact, the country's economic collapse would have been a principal contributing factor, if not the catalyst, motivating a political transition. The corollary to this observation is that the old political regime represented by Castroism will be broadly and directly regarded as responsible for the country's economic deterioration. Intuitively, societal consensus will exist for politico-economic reforms. However, the proposition that the nation as a whole will be psychologically prepared and amenable to the implementation of profound and painful economic reforms does not mean that a popular consensus will exist on precisely what reform measures are required.

The answer to the question of how do economic and political liberalization interact is that " ... fundamentally, where the old political system is widely regarded as an intrinsic source of the nation's economic difficulties, economic reforms without political reforms lack credibility."[103] Economic reforms without political representation fail to provide the channels of interaction between government and civil society at a time when both will be changing rapidly. The simultaneity of political and economic reforms is essential to develop credibility and the precarious balance between societal participatory pressures and the required economic reforms.

---

102 Nelson, Joan M. "The Politics of Economic Transformation: Is Third World Experience Relevant in Eastern Europe?" *World Politics* 45. April 1993, pp. 433–63.

103 Ibid., p. 443

For better or worse, during some of the Central and Eastern European transitions, the central government's authority was often weakened by endless parliamentary debates about specific reform policies, political philosophies, the power of the executive, and more. This inability of amorphous political parties and legislatures to formulate cohesive reform programs and exercise leadership led to a sort of interim deference to and acceptance of technocratic leadership. Paradoxically, rather than policy paralysis, the leadership vacuum and inchoate party platforms were filled by reform-minded technocrats and specialists allowing some governments to implement major economic reforms while in political disarray. Contrary to expectations and to the old belief that authoritarian regimes are best suited to carry out market-oriented reforms, contemporary research and practice in the politics of economic reforms shows that fragmentation of power within post-communist countries has not impeded economic liberalization.

A key feature of the Union of Soviet Socialistic Republics (USSR) was the fusion of political and economic power to promote and facilitate economic self-sufficiency. A prerequisite condition in this pursuit of autarky was that political power and economic policymaking needed to be highly centralized, residing primarily in a small group of elites. These elites, exercising concentrated power, were well-placed to engage in corrupt rent-seeking activities since society at large was unable to check on their activities. Similarly, regimes such as Castro's Cuba, with highly concentrated elites endowed with autocratic powers, are unlikely to engage in reforms that may end their rent-seeking activities.

In a study of twenty-five post-communist countries, researchers Timothy Frye and Edward D. Mansfield find " … the fragmentation of power within post-Communist countries has been a potent force for trade liberalization. In non-democracies where political power is highly concentrated in the hands of a small group of elites, state leaders face few impediments to maintaining the protectionist remnants of Communist rule and are well insulated from interests favoring commercial reform."[104] In contrast, the authors note that the

104 Frye, Timothy and Mansfield, Edward D. "Fragmenting Protection: The Political Economy of Trade Policy in the Post-Communist World." *Cambridge*

dispersion of power characteristic of democracies, together with greater accountability work as a strong force for trade liberalization.

Post-Castro Cuba will inherit a highly concentrated political system, protectionist trade policies, an irrational monetary system, an inhospitable climate for foreign direct investments, and all the other characteristics of centrally planned, mercantilist economies. It will also inherit an enormous technical-bureaucratic apparatus of dreadfully low productivity and efficiency. The somewhat counterintuitive conclusion that the prospects for economic liberalization are not unduly hampered by a degree of power fragmentation flows from the fact that fragmentation creates political space for groups with an interest in liberalization to influence policy outcomes. Economic reforms are promoted when the various constituencies are able to monitor government officials and limit the extent to which public officials are unimpeded to engage in rent-seeking behavior; the greater the ability of society to monitor and penalize government officials for the mismanagement of economic affairs, the better the prospects for genuine liberalization reforms.

This general discussion of how political and economic liberalization will interact in post-Castro Cuba has sought to make two major points. First, there is no such thing as a "non-political decision." The politicization of every economic liberalizing policy is unavoidable, but not necessarily undesirable. Second, the discussion has sought to discredit the old argument that authoritarianism with its centralized power will be necessary to implement market-reforms in Cuba. Bluntly put, no messianic leaders are needed.

From the Bottom Up

A deeper principle underlying the preceding discussion and the one to follow is that economies are best structured from the bottom up and not from the top down. In other words, economies are best structured

University Press, B.J. Pol. S. 33. 2003, pp. 635–657.

as consumer-driven and not as producer-driven. A country's economic output is the product of human action, not of human design. The political equivalency is that the bottom-up democratic engagement of the citizenry is far preferable to autocratic top-down policymaking. The idea that in order for a nation to achieve prosperity, the government must run the economy from the top down should have died an honorable death in 1776, when Adam Smith published "The Wealth of Nations." Unfortunately, mercantilist themes in various forms survive to this day and have permeated Cuban economic thinking since the foundation of the republic.

In essence, mercantilists argue that governments should play a protectionist role in the economy, using tariffs and subsidies to encourage exports and discourage imports. Mercantilism views economic activity as a zero-sum game in which any gains by one party require a loss by another. Although most mainstream economists today reject the core mercantilist principles, the zero-sum game theme remains ingrained in popular thinking. In fairness, the simple, straightforward mercantilist belief that a set of economic policies that benefits one group must inevitably come at the expense of another group has some commonsense (but erroneous) appeal. The logical fallacies of mercantilism and the principles of new wealth creation or comparative advantage are not readily discernible by unreasoned common sense.

Mercantilism, as the dominant school of economic though from the sixteenth to the eighteenth century, led to some of the early instances of significant government interventions and control of national economic activities. Modern quasi-manifestations of mercantilist principles are detectable in interventionist government policies centered on the premise that assigning a government with a "virtuous" task magically fills that activity with intrinsic effectiveness and fairness. Free-market economic reforms in post-Castro Cuba must derive from the more esoteric and counterintuitive principles of *laissez faire* where the creation of new wealth is possible and economic interchanges are not bound as zero-sum games.

It is important to make these points because Cubans have become highly dependent on the government for their subsistence, and because "there is a widespread view that any reforming government will have to satisfy the aspirations of the Cuban people with regard to (i) the provision of public goods and services and (ii) the maintenance of the degree of social and economic equality achieved by the present government."[105] It is understandable that most Cubans would want to continue to receive the social benefits that they may have received under Castroism (i.e., pensions, education, and health). It is also true that " ... the welfare functions of the socialist state are the ones that will leave the most positive collective memories after the change of system."[106] But Castro's Cuba provision of these social benefits deteriorated badly with the discontinuation of Soviet subsidies and has certainly lost some luster in the eyes of the population. By transition time, the peak-end rule will be fully in place (with the emphasis on the end state), and the collective memories will not be nearly as positive. In any case, it will be necessary to demonstrate that nations and citizens do not compete for a fixed amount of wealth in a zero-sum game and that the creation of new wealth is possible.

One non-didactic way of demonstrating to the citizenry the power of economic liberalization, as will be argued below, is to sequence reforms from the bottom up by encouraging the trust-based, reciprocally beneficial exchanges of free-markets that contribute to the creation of a civil society. That is, by empowering individuals and refraining from postulating the banal mercantilist *raison d'état* so overused by Castroism. Top-down mercantilism presented by reasons of state does not contribute to economic prosperity, and just as importantly, it does not contribute to the creation of a more trusting and trustworthy society. The self-reinforcing cycle of free-markets is one in which bottom-up economic interchanges lead to trust and cooperation. It creates what social scientists label a complex adaptive system that learns as it develops. Expanding the autonomous bases for free-market economic activities creates an environment in which Cuban civil society can step forward and evolve.

---

105 Hernández-Catá, Ernesto, p. 22.

106 Kornai, Janos. *What can Countries Embarking on Post-Socialist Transformation Learn from the Experiences so Far?* Miami. Cuba Transition Project. 2004, p. 24.

The General Argument: Gradualism or "Big Bang"

The transition of former communist countries to market economies has been one of the most analyzed economic events of the past twenty years, yet there is no well-established theory of transition or consensus on the best approach. The objective of this chapter on economic reforms is not to revisit the extensive literature on post-communist economic transitions and its many subtopics. The idea here is to select a handful of economic policymaking topics to illustrate how choice architecture principles may be used to induce better governance and the coherent integration of government and the citizenry. Much of what follows is based on the works of prominent Cuban-American economists such as Antonio Jorge, Carmelo Mesa Lago, Ernesto Hernández-Catá, Sergio Diaz-Briquets, Jorge Pérez-López, and others who have produced an intellectually rich and enormously useful output of works related to Cuban and Cuban-American studies.

In general, the prescriptive literature on post-communist economic transitions breaks into two conflicting approaches: one camp emphasizes the gradual, studied sequencing of reforms, while the other camp favors a fast-paced, comprehensive introduction of all elements that constitute a market economy in a "big-bang" approach. Among other things, proponents of the big-bang approach note that new governments should use their political capital window of opportunity to implement the most politically and economically difficult reforms all in one stroke.

In post-Castro Cuba, given that the extrication from the communist regime will hinge on conflict resolution based primarily on bargaining and compromise, the big-bang *in toto* approach appears unlikely. Reformers will be bound by the political constraints of the transition negotiations. In a study of "The Design of Reforms Packages under Uncertainty," the authors argue, "(i) gradualist reform packages have generally higher *ex ante* feasibility and can thus start earlier, and (ii) sequencing of reforms may create constituencies for continuing reforms and increase *ex post* irreversibility of enacted reforms ..."[107] On

---

107 Dewatripont, Mathias and Roland, Gerard. "The Design of Reform Packages under Uncertainty." *American Economic Review.* December 1995, pp. 1207–

the other hand, "A big-bang strategy involves high reversal costs, which are often considered to be an advantage *ex post* since it reduces the reversibility of enacted reforms."[108] However, a big-bang approach may be viewed as politically unfeasible when a negative outcome is possible, and high reversal costs make it very difficult to change course.

In other words, the low reversibility of comprehensive market reforms is a highly desirable feature of the big-bang approach, but gradualism makes reforms easier to start because political actors are less fearful of being locked into an irreversible policy mistake. The authors of this study further argue that correct sequencing can foment momentum and strengthen the political support for additional reforms. In contrast, incorrect sequencing that begins with the most painful reforms may undermine popular support.

The case for gradualism is thus anchored on the correct sequencing of reforms and their tempo. There is no question that gradualism increases the political viability of reforms. But it is essential to consider who is conducting the reforms. Gradualism conducted by a former communist nomenklatura imbued with their peculiar zero-sum mind set and operating without a well-specified transition blueprint would only exacerbate venality and rent-seeking behavior. Gradualism in the wrong hands can become the enemy of legitimate reforms.

Rather than framing Cuba's economic reform program in terms of gradualist or big-bang comprehensive approaches, the transition model should seek to harmonize politics and economics organically in a way conducive to the development of Cuba's civil society. Cuba's economic situation is desperate, and it should be clear that a total systemic change is required. In the end, the entire maze of irrational organizations, norms, and institutions must be abandoned to engender a new polity and economy.

It is also clear that an initial macroeconomic liberalization program will be necessary at the very beginning of the transition and that stabilization policies need to be implemented. Beyond that, Cuba will have to proceed recognizing that the process of social change and the methods and tempo of implementation will influence the stability of

---

23.

108 Ibid., p. 1208

the political and social orders. In the comments below, the standard economic gradualism vs. big bang debate will be left behind in favor of sketching out a Cuba-specific hybrid approach that seeks rapid, bold changes in some economic spheres and gradualism in others. The comprehensive objective is to bring about the healthiest, strongest development of the private sector consistent with and overseen by democratic values and democratic governance.

The First Big Steps

The initial post-Castro Cuban economic condition will be one of extreme, desperate impoverishment coupled with a badly damaged social fabric and an extraordinary degree of unproductivity. The "Comparative Analysis of Purchasing Power in Cuba" below shows succinctly in dramatic, comparative fashion the low purchasing power of Cuban workers. [109]

---

109 Gonzalez-Corzo, Mario A. and Perez, Susel. "Comparative Analysis of Purchasing Power in Cuba." Miami. Institute for Cuban and Cuban-American Studies. May 2009.

Table 1. Comparative Analysis of the Purchasing Power of the Average Worker by Country, Selected Data, November 2008					
Consumer Basket (CB)		**Hours of Work Required to Purchase the Items in the CB**			
Product Description	**Unit**	**Cuba**	**Costa Rica**	**Honduras**	**Dominican Republic**
Powdered milk, instantaneous	400 gr. Box	57.5	1.7	5.4	11.4
Fresh, boneless chicken	Pound	15.8	2.1	1.8	4.5
Prime, fresh pork rib	Pound	20.5	1.9	3.0	7.6
White, fresh, eggs	Dozen	6.0	0.3	2.5	5.0
Rice	Pound	3.2	0.4	1.0	2.0
Yellow onion, medium size	Pound	7.5	0.3	0.9	3.8
White potato, fresh	Pound	8.5	0.3	0.9	2.3
Ripe plantain, medium size	Unit	1.7	0.2	0.1	1.3

This table shows, for example, that to purchase a 400-gram box of powdered milk, the average Cuban worker has to sacrifice 57.5 hours (7.2 days) of work. To make the same purchase, the average worker in Costa Rica has to work only 1.7 hours (.18 days). Similarly, to purchase a pound of fresh, boneless chicken, the average Cuban worker has to dedicate close to two days of work (15.8 hours), compared to only 2.1 hours for the average Costa Rican worker. Comparable inefficiencies hold for the other items in the consumer basket analyzed in this study.

The low purchasing power of the Cuban worker follows from the gross inefficiencies that characterize the Cuban centrally planned economy, but also from the existence of a dual monetary system. Under the Cuban system, workers are paid in pesos (CUPs), but goods are available mostly in the state-run hard currency stores and in the informal market sector that require the use of convertible pesos (CUCs). Ironically, this monetary dualism has contributed to an increase in inequality between Cubans with access to hard currency (e.g., from the remittances of family members outside Cuba or those employed in the tourist sector) and Cubans without access to hard currencies—mostly Afro-Cubans. Surveys of Cubans on the island show that the dual-currency system is the single most detested economic policy of the communist economic system. The dual monetary system has no supporting constituency in the Cuban population.

From a political perspective, this broad-based hatred of the dual-monetary system opens up an opportunity for a reforming post-Castro government to act boldly and quickly to implement two of the most painful and far-reaching macroeconomic reforms: the liberalization of prices and the unification of the exchange system. The implementation of these two key structural macroeconomic adjustments does not fall in the gradualist camp and should precede, not follow, other measures such as privatization. Price liberalization and a rational and stable exchange rate are precursors that make private initiative possible. Prices have to be freed from arbitrary controls so that they can accurately signal relative scarcities for the private sector to act on. Without a single, stable currency, perverse incentives will prevail and will impede economic efficiency. The dual-currency system disrupts labor and capital markets and creates obstacles for the integration of the domestic and external economies. The abrupt unification of the currency system would create adjustment difficulties in the short term, but would set the stage for economic dynamism going forward.

The debate as to what should happen to firms and other assets in state ownership (the privatization debate) should be guided by a much more important principle than considerations of sequencing and methods. The guiding principle should be to act quickly and boldly to bring about a healthy, rapid, and strong development of the country's private sector, overseen by democratic values and governance while minimizing bureaucratic opportunism and malfeasance.

The argument that prioritizes economic measures, even if undertaken outside the framework of democratic governance, fails to recognize that private entrepreneurs in those circumstances would remain highly dependent on the arbitrariness of government officials. Entrepreneurs working in undemocratic settings do not mobilize for political reforms that would antagonize their "partners" in the government's bureaucracy. The often-cited case of China makes this point. There is no evidence that China's new entrepreneurial class sought to ally themselves with the student protesters during the 1989 pro-democracy movement. In fact, it is possible to make the opposite case that this opportunistic entrepreneurial class under a totalitarian regime is so dependent on the regime's decision making that they would not jeopardize their financial wellbeing by supporting anti-regime movements.

The discussion will return to privatization and related issues latter, but let's first consider below—in the spirit of a thought-provoking polemicist—the question of the most appropriate exchange rate regime for post-Castro Cuba.

The "Dollarization" Option

Arguably, from a purely economic point of view, a managed float approach to exchange rates, together with a meticulously independent central bank formulating and conducting monetary policy, offers significant advantages. But the transition architects in post-Castro Cuba will need to employ the imaginative approaches of choice architecture to accomplish key goals that go beyond pure economic rationality. The dollarization of the Cuban economy offers one such controversial approach.

Since the end of the Bretton Woods system of fixed exchange rates, independent nations have faced a variety of choices regarding the decision about which exchange rate regime to adopt. The topic is broad, controversial, and complex. The treatment here is Cuba-specific, and technically superficial. Full dollarization (or dollarization, for short) refers to a country officially abandoning its own currency and adopting the currency of another for all financial transactions (expect perhaps for coins).

In the political realm, countries are reluctant to abandon their own currencies, which are often a symbol of nationhood. Historically, political opposition to dollarization (the term is used here as a shorthand expression for the adoption of any foreign currency, as the South African rand was in that region) has been strong. However, since the adoption of the euro by a significant number of European countries, this chauvinistic tendency may have ameliorated. In any case, the main attraction of dollarization is the elimination of the risk associated with a sudden devaluation of a country's exchange rate. Devaluation is a condition that, in addition to raising borrowing costs, also wreaks havoc on the economies of developing countries. Dollarization allows developing countries to reduce the risk premium attached to their international borrowing.

It should be mentioned that the stability offered by dollarization is relative, given that all hard currencies, including the dollar, will fluctuate in value against other widely traded currencies. Also, while dollarization will eliminate the risk premium owing to devaluation risk, it does not eliminate the risk premium attached to sovereign risk. Notwithstanding these caveats, for developing countries, "an immediate benefit from eliminating the risk of devaluation is reducing the country risk premium on foreign borrowing and obtaining lower interest rates for the government and private sector. Lower interest rates and more stability in international capital movements cut the cost of servicing public debt, and encourage higher investment and economic growth."[110]

---

110 Berg, Andrew and Borensztein, Eduardo. "Full Dollarization: The Pros and Cons." *IMF Economic Issues* No. 24. December 2000. http://www.imf.org/external/pubs/ft/issues/issues24/index.htm

A tradeoff for the lower interest rates on foreign borrowing is that a country adopting dollarization gives up the revenue that flows from *seigniorage*.[111] That is, a country adopting a foreign currency as legal tender sacrifices its *seigniorage*—the profits accruing to the monetary authority from its right to issue currency with a face value higher than its production costs.

The adoption of dollarization in post-Castro Cuba would entail a perhaps unaffordable "stock" cost. As the dollar is introduced and the domestic currency withdrawn from circulation, the monetary authorities must buy back the stock of domestic currency held by the population. Cuba would not have sufficient foreign reserves to buy back its domestic currency and would have to borrow the necessary reserves. If post-Castro Cuba is engaged in a legitimate, transparent transition to democracy and free markets, this need not be an insurmountable problem, as the United States, other nations, and international institutions could be persuaded to grant credits for this specific purpose.

In fact, since dollarization means that the United States would get more *seigniorage* from the dollarization of the Cuban economy, it could be persuaded to share part or all of the additional *seigniorage* revenues with Cuba. The powerful and influential Cuban-American political community could lobby the U.S. Congress to consider legislation providing for *seigniorage* reimbursement. The United States does not currently have such a sharing policy; however, a precedent for *seigniorage* reimbursement exists in the arrangement between South Africa and Lesotho, Namibia, and Swaziland, the three other states that use the South African rand as their national currency.

Post-Castro Cuba would have a desperate need to gain monetary stability. Initially, the absence of credible independent institutions, the country's huge external debt, and its disastrous domestic economy make this stability an impossible task. Dollarization is a method of importing someone else's monetary stability. An additional major benefit of

---

111 The ancient concept of seigniorage refers to a government profit from issuing coinage that costs less to mint than its face value. The concept is essentially the same for paper currencies.

dollarization is that it would facilitate greater economic integration with the United States, Cuba's natural trade partner, as well as with the rest of the world. Dollarization will help to establish a firm basis for a sound financial sector and thus help promote economic growth. To some degree, a democratically transitioning Cuba will experience a de facto dollarization, as dollars from the Cuban-American community, as well as from American tourists and enterprises, would flow to the island, a phenomenon not unlike the dollars that found their way to Europe after World War II.

Perhaps the strongest argument against dollarization is that the country would give up some important monetary policy tools, since the absence of a central bank prevents monetary interventions. However, for post-Castro Cuba, this may also be the strongest argument for dollarization. The absence of a central bank means that the government would not be able to monetize its deficits by printing money. Dollarization would impose effective, hard budget constraints on the government. Without the ability to print money, the government would be limited in its ability to function as a lender of last resort for inefficient state enterprises. In short, dollarization would induce the government to act with a degree of fiscal prudence and discipline. For outside investors, risks are reduced because they do not have to be concerned with the risks of government policy decisions regarding monetary exchange affairs. Dollarization provides for lower business transaction costs and stability of prices in dollar terms. It also creates a positive sentiment for domestic and international investors.

It was noted above that devaluation and instability wreak havoc on the economies of developing countries. At a microeconomic level, these conditions weigh heavily on business planning and on the time horizons of investors. Devaluation and instability concerns by the business community may help to explain why historically Cuban and Latin American entrepreneurs have prioritized short-term profits over long term profitability. This short-term business time horizon predates Castroism. For instance, a World Bank team that visited Cuba in 1950 concluded that "too many private employers were 'static' or 'defensive' in their business approach seeking immediate profits rather than investing for the long term."[112] Entrepreneurship *mañana* in Cuba must be nudged to favor investing for the long run rather than speculative short-term profit taking. Stability in general and currency stability in particular are necessary to promote long-term entrepreneurial thinking and extended planning horizons.

In theory, a flexible exchange rate may be optimal for post-Castro Cuba. But the high probability of mismanagement of exchange rate or monetary policy is an ever-present danger in a politically charged transition situation. Dollarization is not necessarily a policy straightjacket. Government does have other ways of financing deficits, e.g., borrowing. It is, however, not only a very effective nudge toward financial prudence and discipline in government expending, but also a near-irreversible policy step in the right direction.

The Stimulation of Entrepreneurial Activity

Hand in hand with the two big macroeconomic steps of the complete liberalization of prices and dollarization, the transition government needs to lift barriers to free enterprise and stimulate private initiative in small and medium-sized enterprises. This includes the quick privatization of small state-owned enterprises. Cuba's redevelopment will not depend so much on the privatization of large, state-owned enterprises—a measure that should follow in short order—but on the renaissance of private business initiative and activity. The expeditious development of the private sector requires the dismantling of the barriers to free market entry. Widespread private ownership is the principal objective. Of course, the proportion of state and collective ownership of productive assets has to decrease to allow private ownership to become the predominant form of ownership. New "greenfield" investments by new market entrants, and not the privatization of large, state-owned enterprises, is what will lead to the spreading of private ownership.

---

112 Gjelten, Tom. *Bacardi and the Long Fight for Cuba*. New York. Viking. 2008, p. 174

On the political side of the equation, privatization methods (to be discussed below) will be controversial and time consuming as the various methods, valuation approaches, and the like are discussed and stakeholders seek to influence the process. On the other hand, the freeing of the population's entrepreneurial spirit to stimulate domestic "greenfield" business activity is a no-brainer that is not going to develop serious political opposition. Moreover, in an environment of market-determined prices where real production costs and consumer preferences predominate, many investors would find starting a new production facility to be simpler and more economic than updating an inefficient state-owned facility.

One reason for initiating a competitive market economy and promoting new business activity prior to undertaking the privatization of large, state-owned enterprises is that some will not survive the competitive environment. Many of Cuba's chronically inefficient enterprises, if unable to receive government subsidies (due to the dollarization of the economy) may simply collapse into bankruptcy. A hidden (or not so hidden) agenda of dollarization is that it imposes hard budgetary constraints on state-owned enterprises. The choice architecture embodied in dollarization performs for politicians the difficult and unpopular job of weaning out the subsidies of state enterprises that survive only under soft budgetary arrangements. To be clear, the enterprises in question are already de facto bankrupt. They operate only by being artificially propped up by state subsidies. Dollarization and the market economy are not the causal agents of their demise. Market forces will only reveal their status for all to see, a sort of privatization via bankruptcy.

The privatization of state-owned enterprises is often viewed as the centerpiece of post-communist transitions, a status that is reflected in the extensive scholarly literature that examines the various approaches to privatization employed by the transitioning countries of Central and Eastern Europe. Of particular relevance to post-Castro Cuba are studies by Cuban-Americans and other specialists under the auspices of the University of Miami's Cuba Transition Project.[113] These monographs

---

113 The Cuba Transition Project, at the Institute for Cuban and Cuban-American

discuss in detail the complex political and socioeconomic issues enveloping the privatization of state-owned enterprises via direct sales, voucher mechanisms, auctions, and more.

The cardinal principles of privatization are that it be carried out transparently, equitably, and without undue delay. Privatization of large, state-owned enterprises must be preceded by a significant degree of institutional reforms. In general, scholars who have studied in depth the experiences of other post-communist transitioning countries seem to agree that direct sales to concentrated outside investors would be in Cuba's best interest. Professor Antonio Jorge notes:

> In the particular case of privatization through the distribution of vouchers to the population at large, the dispersion and weakness of the initial owners will most likely eventuate in control by the colluded interest of financial intermediaries such as investment funds and the banking system ... Clearly then, there are manifold disadvantages to the public auctions and voucher procedures as privatization means. In Cuba's case, given the country's distinct traits, it is incumbent upon the reformers to rely on other methods of privatizing economic activity.[114]

Similarly, Professor Ernesto Hernández-Catá argues:

> As regards privatization, an emphasis on *direct sales* to concentrated outside partners rather than *voucher distribution* would be in Cuba's best interest. Concentrated investors (including foreign companies) have a stronger incentive than "insiders" (management/workers) to maximize long-term profits, to align their interests with

---

Studies (ICCAS), University of Miami, is an important and timely project to study and make recommendations for the reconstruction of Cuba once the post-Castro transition begins in earnest. The project started in January 2002 and is funded by a grant from the U.S. Agency for International Development.

114 Jorge, Antonio. *Privatization, Reconstruction, and Socio-Economic Development in Post-Castro Cuba*. Miami. Cuba Transition Project. 2003, p. 18.

those of minority owners, to avoid assets stripping, and to provide capital and market experience."[115]

In other words, selling off state-owned assets at a fair price to those most likely to put them to effective productive use is the most practical alternative from both economic and ethical points of view.

A very closely related topic to privatization is the thorny problems associated with the reprivatization of expropriated properties. As a matter of ethics and law, property claims by Cuban and U.S. nationals must be addressed by any post-Castro reform government seeking to establish credibility with domestic and foreign investors. Confidence in the very process of privatization demands a resolution to the property claims on Cuban state property resulting from its expropriations after 1959. This is an extremely complex problem that does not lend itself to any completely just solution.

Fundamentally, there are two generic options: physical restitution and indemnification. Physical restitution, although it does have strong ethical appeal, cannot be carried out on a timely basis and would not be practical in most cases. But some method of compensation must be offered to former owners, perhaps in the form of Cuban government securities. Notwithstanding the compensation modality, the essential principle is to reestablish respect for property rights. Property rights have to be firmly established under the rule of law in order to lay the foundation for a market-based economy.

Clearly, the feasibility of any particular approach to privatization will be subject to the political climate at the time of privatization and on the institutions in place to carry out the process. In economic terms, privatization is simply the exchange of one asset class for another, but politically it is much more than that. From the perspective developed throughout this work, it is essential that the privatization of large, state-owned enterprises be as much of an at-arm's-length process as possible. Any perceived sense of illegitimacy would be highly detrimental to public trust, which is the core building block for the development of Cuba's civil society.

---

115 Hernández-Catá, Ernesto. Op cit, p. i.

Government Revenue Sources

With a dollarized economy imposing significant constraints on government expenditures, post-Castro Cuba will be compelled to reduce the massive state apparatus. At the same time, price liberalization and dollarization will require increases in public sector salaries, pension, and other safety net expenses to help protect the purchasing power of the population in dollar terms. Policies of austerity, stabilization, and liberalization will foster a difficult social climate. The transitioning government will confront many policy tradeoffs in the allocation of resources. A danger is that the transition government will seek to raise its revenues from taxation policies that will work at cross purposes with the promotion of economic growth and development.

In general, personal income taxes based on earned income, as used in the United States, have proven to be unenforceable in most developing countries and certainly would not be appropriate in early post-Castro Cuba on several grounds. Of particular concern here is that such taxes where trust in government institutions is very low would result in all sorts of avoidance tactics, undermining the development of a culture of law. The joke is told that when income tax rates are increased in the United States, taxpayers will lose sleep over how to pay the new taxes by cutting expenses, working additional hours, etc. Likewise, the Latin American taxpayer will also lose sleep looking for ways to avoid paying the new taxes. The choice architecture employed for the design of Cuba's tax code should seek to promote law abiding behavior and link, in the minds of the citizens, tax payments with government services.

Some developing countries faced with the need for ongoing government revenues, but unable to enforce broad-based personal income tax systems, have targeted easy to collect taxes such as import duties and tariffs. While a low level of non-preferential tariff is a legitimate source of easily collectible government revenue, over-reliance on such mechanisms is not consistent with open trade policies and economic development. In any case, from a free-market perspective, taxing personal income (particularly in a progressive fashion) is not necessarily the most philosophically coherent method of raising government revenues. Penalizing the economic success of the personal initiatives that are being promoted as the key vehicle for economic growth is philosophically inconsistent.

Post-Castro Cuba's guiding principles for taxation need to steer clear of promoting distortions in resource allocation decisions to avoid weakening the personal initiatives of entrepreneurs on which the reconstruction process hinges. Taxation policies also need to be designed with an eye to fostering respect for the law and promoting an understanding of how government revenues are used to finance essential government functions. With these goals in mind, the best personal taxation approach to promote a democratic, participatory, free-market Cuba would be a very simple (and simple to enforce) broad-based sales tax without exceptions or preferences, except possibly for basic food items. Ideally, a consumption-based sales tax would have a high compliance rate, be difficult to avoid, and be simple to calculate and collect.

In developed countries, the debate over consumption-based sales taxes focuses on their presumed regressivity. As the argument goes, a sales tax would be regressive because lower-income households would spend a greater percentage of their income in taxable purchases than higher-income households. Of course, this particular calculation is based on an arbitrary decision to relate the tax to income. An alternative calculation relating the tax to expenditures would yield that those who consume more pay more taxes.

It is not clear that these developed countries' arguments would resonate in Cuba. By and large, transitioning Cuba will consist primarily of low-income households (the presumed equality of a communist country), where the argument that sales taxes unfairly target the poor is somewhat of a moot point. Notwithstanding these considerations, the principal reason to advocate a simple sales tax responds to different reasoning. It follows the principles of transparency and using every possible choice architecture opportunity to increase the coherence between government and the governed. A highly visible sales tax on purchases tells the citizenry exactly how much their government is costing them in a very personal, timely, and direct way. It is one more mechanism to nudge the citizenry to assume responsibility for their governance and to build a civil society.

Nudging Foreign Direct Investments

The international movements of capital are a vital component of the global economy. Reformers and investors will find in post-Castro Cuba a decapitalized country in acute need of capital and expertise. The critical need for foreign capital and expertise in the reconstruction of post-communist economies was colorfully captured by Poland's President Walesa: "I want the United States to send me its best generals: General Electric, General Motors, and General Mills."

However, an unfounded popular belief exists that a post-Castro, post-embargo Cuba will attract massive investments and will result in a business bonanza for American companies. Observers point out that after more than fifty years of totalitarian rule and a failed command economic system, Cuba and its population of over eleven million are in desperate need of practically any product and service conceivable. But, as would be expected, capital flows toward the most attractive investment countries and projects, and a more critical examination of Cuba's ability to attract U.S. foreign direct investment (FDI) in a post-Castro milieu yields a different conclusion.[116]

From the point of view of the strategic choices of firms that will be weighted by corporate executives, need or market size alone will not justify an FDI commitment. Typically, firms seek to mitigate international risks by starting with low risk/low cost market entry options, such as exporting, and advancing to higher levels of risk and control (FDI) only if beneficial to the firm and/or competitively necessary.

Certainly, in a post-embargo environment, U.S. companies will want to export their goods and services to Cuba. From a corporate perspective, exports (foreign sales) are the preferred entry method for a company to serve a market such as Cuba, while minimizing business and political risks. But exports by U.S. companies to Cuba will not directly contribute the capital, technology transfers, and other desirable

---

116 For a more comprehensive discussion of these topics see: Azel, José "Cuban-Americans and Foreign Direct Investments in Post-Castro Cuba: "An Ace in the Hole." *Cuban Affairs Quarterly Electronic Journal.* Vol. 3.1, January 2008.

components of direct investments that will be so desperately needed in post-Castro Cuba. A firm looking to sell to Cuba is not equivalent to a firm investing in Cuba.

Generally, firms invest in a foreign market to (1) gain access to a location specific natural resource such as oil or minerals—resource-seeking investments; (2) to establish feeder plants to take advantage of lower local production costs—efficiency-seeking investments; or (3) to supply the local market—market-seeking investments. Regarding the first resource-seeking type of FDI, Cuba will indeed attract the interest of U.S. companies, particularly in oil, nickel, agriculture, and tourism. Even under the very unfavorable conditions for FDI prevalent in the Castro era, some international companies have sought to invest in these areas.

But, with an abundance of low-labor-cost countries around the globe that firms can choose for efficiency-seeking investments, it is unlikely that Cuba will be able to attract this type of FDI. The Cuban labor force, after more than five decades of operating in a command economy system, is ill equipped for the demanding labor requirements of a modern market economy. Comparatively speaking, Cuba does not offer U.S. companies seeking lower labor costs a compelling reason to invest in the country.

In terms of market-seeking FDI, Cuba may appear to offer a meaningful opportunity. But Cuba represents an impoverished market with minimal disposable or discretionary income. Second, when compared to the populations of large countries such as China or India, Cuba's comparative market size does not rate highly enough to be selected for an FDI geared to supply the local market. Third, Cuba's internal market may be inadequate to support investments in production facilities that require a much larger consumer base in order to achieve the necessary economies of scale. Fourth, production in a Cuba-based facility will be handicapped by having to import many, if not most, of the components and parts required in the production process, as few will be available from Cuban production sources. Finally, and perhaps most importantly, U.S. companies, if they are able to export their goods to Cuba, will elect exports as a much lower-cost and lower-risk market serving strategy.

Therefore, from the vantage point of corporate executives, there is no reason to expect that U.S. firms will rush to invest in a post-embargo Cuba. This remains the case even if we postulate a best-case scenario where a smooth democratic and market-based transition is taking place, and the Cuban government is policy-friendly toward U.S. investors. Given this discouraging outlook, what steps can be taken by a future Cuban transition government interested in attracting FDI and a U.S. administration wanting to encourage or nudge American companies to invest in a democratic Cuba?

Both on the U.S. and the Cuban side one approach anchored on the principles of business strategy is to foster a *competitive urgency* to invest in a democratic, market-oriented Cuba. Choice architecture principles can be employed to reward first-moving firms with a substantial and sustainable competitive advantage. In business strategic planning, the concept of competitive advantage calls for cost-effective efforts to alter a company's strength relative to that of its competitors. For companies, the strategic value of a competitive advantage depends on its sustainability. Sustainability, in turn, exists if competitors find it difficult to replicate or imitate the source of a firm's advantage.

For example, in terms of policy formulation, a creative package of tax exemptions, deferrals, duty-free access to the U.S. market, and other incentives can be made available only to those firms that have established a production facility in Cuba by a given date, say within two or three years after the embargo has been lifted. The idea behind this timing provision is to utilize an institutional entry barrier to provide sustainability to first-moving firms. This tactic provides first-moving firms with a substantial and sustainable competitive advantage over competitors that choose not to invest by the sunset date. In the competitive environment created by such a policy, a Cuba-based facility becomes a *compelling competitive necessity* in order to avoid a disadvantageous position.

Additionally, a post-Castro Cuba will have access to an exceptional country-specific comparative advantage: the Cuban-American community. In terms of facilitating FDI in Cuba, Cuban-Americans can play a pivotal role, not only as entrepreneurs owning small and medium-sized businesses, but also as executives working in large national and multinational enterprises. For post-Castro Cuba, the capital and skill sets of the Cuban-American community represent a comparative advantage unlike that of any other country competing for U.S. foreign direct investment.

Cuban-Americans, for the most part, will not be hindered by the innate disadvantages of foreignness, and their investment decision-making will not be bound by strict economic rationality. The investment decisions of Cuban-Americans will be based on a different and very personal risk-reward analysis, and many will seek to invest for reasons totally unrelated to resource, efficiency, or market-seeking motives. Moreover, in a transition setting lacking a modern legal system conducive to sophisticated contractual arrangements, a Cuban-American businessperson will be more amenable to entering into formal or informal contractual arrangements with a Cuban partner than, say, a publicly traded U.S. company.

Typically, in U.S. businesses, someone within the corporate structure has to "carry the flag" for a particular project. Someone has to be a "champion" who persuades other executives of the wisdom of a given course of action. This is precisely the role that Cuban-American executives can perform within the U.S. corporate world; they can carry the flag for their companies' Cuban FDI venture. Thus both as entrepreneurs and as corporate executives, Cuban-Americans can be FDI first-mover catalysts.

A future Cuban transition government needs to set aside whatever hostility it may harbor for Cuban-Americans and employ the conceptual sophistication to recognize that their exceptional skill sets will be essential for the island's speedy economic reconstruction. There may indeed be some economic opportunism at play, but many successful entrepreneurs and executives in the Cuban-American community also feel duty-bound to contribute whatever skills they may possess to the reconstruction of their homeland. To a post-Castro Cuban transition government seeking to attract U.S. FDI, Cuban-Americans represent its "ace in the hole" —a hidden advantage or resource kept in reserve until needed, an opportunity to turn failure into success.

Chapter XIII – Concluding Thoughts

The heart has its reasons of which reason knows nothing.

Blaise Pascal

As THESE REFLECTIONS GO TO press, it has been fifty-one years since that January in 1959 when the Cuban Revolution, like the circus, came to town. But unlike the circus, it stayed for an extended engagement. Over half a century of living and learning as a Cuban outside Cuba has not only shaped my personal beliefs regarding the role that freedoms play in our lives, but the exile experience has also strengthened the bonds with a nation I know experientially only as an adolescent.

Nationhood is not a place, but an ethnic identity, and Cubans in exile are best understood as a nation without a state. In political geography, an exclave is defined as a territory legally belonging to a country while being geographically enveloped by another country. Culturally, the Cuban exile community is an exclave that remains emotionally attached to Cuba independently of its place of residence. It is a nation that, with the passing of time, has not lost its Cuban identity and has become more ideologically committed to personal freedoms and empowerment. It is an exiled nation well placed to be a positive factor in Cuba's transition.

The lesson learned in exile is that the unarticulated social experiences of countless individuals empowered to exercise free choices are a far better guide to governance than the articulated rationality of messianic philosopher-kings. Moreover, individual freedoms and empowerment are essential to live meaningful lives. It is crucial to always remember, "No matter how ferocious the onslaught of a totalitarian state, history has demonstrated that civil society does mange to survive, although often in greatly reduced numbers, sometimes in minimal cells."[117] The independent spirit of a population somehow manages to endure. Such is the case with the Cuban nation today. Yoani Sanchez writes of offering a smile as a stab of delight that cuts and pierces those who do not know how to handle the unexpected joy of the captive.

Active, public resistance to totalitarian ideology in Cuba today is limited to a compact community with an intense internal dynamic that carries on a non-violent asymmetrical confrontation with an absolutely repressive regime. Thus these reflections are full of tension between national faith and hope for *mañana* in Cuba and a sober analysis of the legacy of Castroism.

Individual freedoms and empowerment are central to the mental comforts that give dignity to human existence. Thus, to reflect cohesively on *mañana* in Cuba, it is necessary to understand that the country's potentialities will be contingent, not just on economic conditions, but on the individual decisions of the many. Social processes function, with other factors, as enabling conditions. Transitologists tend to emphasize the instruments of transition: economic programs, institution building, investments, capital, and the like. This is a very incomplete picture, since the ultimate determinant of Cuba's transitional path will not be the instruments of transition. These instruments do not exist independently of society. Ultimately, the effectiveness of Cuba's transition will be determined by the society that employs the instruments rather than the instruments themselves.

For *mañana* in Cuba, this means that any economic changes that do not *ex ante* place individual freedoms and empowerment front and center via pluralistic, free, and fair elections would condemn Cuban society to live a provisional existence of unknown limit, to continue living a provisional existence that wounds the human spirit and does

---

117 Gutiérrez-Boronat, Orlando. Op cit. p. 164

not promote the development of democratic sociopolitical values. Individuals who cannot see the end of their provisional existence are not able to aim for life's ultimate goals. They experience an existence without a future and without a goal. They cannot become the citizens who will sustain a democratic state.

Political rights and civil liberties are not superfluous luxuries to be appended to a program of economic reforms. Political rights and civil liberties are the very essence of progress that allow an empowered citizenry to correct mistakes, voice discontent, and bring about changes in leadership. As Nobel Prize-winning Indian economist Amartya Sen has written, "People in economic need also need a political voice. Democracy is not a luxury that can await the arrival of general prosperity." Cuban Communism cannot be reformed to bring about a genuine transition with democratically acceptable results. It is not sufficient to introduce some market reforms in a command economy system. A new, pluralistic, intellectual paradigm is needed. And that democratic paradigm will not be forthcoming from an elite whose governing modality is ontologically inseparable from Cuba's current state of affairs. Democracy requires a relationship model between the state and its citizens that is dramatically different from the relationship model of a Marxist-Leninist state.

It is not just that profound structural reforms must be undertaken in the political and economic domains, but that it is essential to discard the despotic notion that the "special knowledge" of the few should rule the activities of the many. This is a notion that leads necessarily to the predatory premise that rewards should be ultimately determined and controlled by the political power of the few. In contrast, post-Castro Cuba needs to learn to value the role of the individual and their commitment to civic virtues more than ever. Democracy is, in and of itself, a good of the highest value. It is a supra-ideological good, not an ornamental one. Democracy will fail when there is no appreciation for its decisive role or a clear intent to build a democratic government and society.

El Silencio Otorga (Silence Grants Consent)

For decades, Cubans have been taught that others (e.g., the United States) are responsible for the country's underdevelopment and that an enlightened messianic leader was necessary to deliver them from their plight. As a society, Cubans have developed a stasis of conformism. To awaken aspirations, to venture to dream and hope, to escape its daily Sisyphean tasks, Cuban society must exorcise the mythology of the messianic maximum leader and attain a measure of sociopolitical mental health. This cannot take place within a Kafkaesque bureaucracy of absurd, disorienting, menacing complexity. It cannot take place within a regime of authoritarian continuity masquerading as a regime of change, a regime that has reduced citizens to a childlike passivity and dependency.

The new Cuban discourse must be one that explains that the root causes of prosperity and development are to be found in the principles of liberal democracy and the rule of law. These are principles that are inherently irreconcilable with authoritarian rule by the few. Friedrich A. Hayek in "Law, Legislation and Liberty" quotes a communist writer who affirms that "communism means not the victory of socialist law, but the victory of socialism over any law."[118]

The most insidious and devastating legacy of Castroism is that Cuban society, living in constant fear, has forgotten how to feel free. Visions of *mañana* in Cuba may differ both morally and intellectually. But promoting a Cuban society that relearns how to feel free should be a common denominator of all *mañana* in Cuba visions. A vision that leaves in place, and relies on, rule by the few necessarily undermines the rule of law and promotes a culture of fear. It sabotages the establishment of strong democratic institutions with the independent power to protect the citizenry against the abuses of state-induced powers. As such, it would continue that infamous complicity of silence that has granted

---

118 F.A. Hayek, Law, Legislation and Liberty, Vol. II, p. 86 as quoted by Thomas Sowell, Kindle location 1808.

consent for the destruction of democratic institutions throughout Cuban history.

It is my hope in sharing these reflections that the complicit societal silence that a ten year old witnessed in 1959 will not return to *mañana* in Cuba and that Cubans will be able to feel always free.

Works Cited

Aguilar León, Luis. *Cuba y su Futuro*. Miami. Ediciones Universal. 1992: 186.

Alonso, Jose F. "The Ochoa Affair and its Aftermath." In Irving Horowitz's *Cuban Communism*. New Jersey, Transaction Publishers. 1998.

Arias King, Fredo. *Transiciones: La Experiencia de Europa Del Este*. Buenos Aires. Fund. Cadal, Fudacion Pontis, and CEON. 2005.

Aslund, Anders. *Russia's Capitalist Revolution*. Washington D.C. Peterson Institute for International Economics. 2007: 80.

Aung San Suu Kyi. *Freedom from Fear*. New York. Penguin Books. 1995: 181

Aung San Suu Kyi, *The Voice of Hope*. New York. Seven Stories Press. 2008: 7

Azel, José. "Cuban-Americans and Foreign Direct Investments in Post-Castro Cuba: An Ace in the Hole." *Cuban Affairs Quarterly Electronic Journal*. Vol. 3.1, January 2008.

Azel, José. "How to Think about Change in Cuba: A guide for Policymakers." *Cuban Affairs Electronic Journal*. 3.3 September 2008.

Berg, Andrew and Eduardo Borensztein. "Full Dollarization: The Pros and Cons." *IMF Economic Issues* No. 24. December 2000. http://www.imf.org/external/pubs/ft/issues/issues24/index.htm

"Change in Cuba: How Citizens View Their Country's Future." *Freedom House*. Special Report. 15 September 2008. http://www.freedomhouse.org/uploads/ChangeinCuba.pdf

"Cuba Hard Currency Debt, 2008." *Cuba Facts*. Issue 47. Cuba Transition Project, Institute for Cuban and Cuban-American Studies. May 2009.

"Cuban Public Opinion Survey." *The International Republican Institute*. 20 June 2008. http://www.iri.org/lac/cuba/pdfs/2008%20June%205%20Survey%20of%20Cuban%20Public%20Opinion,%20March%2014-April%2012,%202008.pdf

Dewatripont, Mathias and Gerard Roland. "The Design of Reform Packages under Uncertainty." *American Economic Review*. December 1995, pp. 1207–23.

Espinosa Chepe, Oscar. "Crisis Sobre Crisis." XIX Conferencia de la Asociacion para el Estudio de la Economía Cubana. 2009.

Fernandez, Damian J. "The Greatest Challenges: Civic Values in Post-Transition Cuba." *Cuba Transition Project*. 2003: 1

Ferreira, Ramon. *Donde está la luz*, as quoted in Perez, Louis A. *To Die in Cuba,* p. 16.

Frankl, Viktor E. *Man's Search for Meaning*. Boston. Beakon Press. 2006.

Frye, Timothy and Mansfield, Edward D. "Fragmenting Protection: The Political Economy of Trade Policy in the Post-Communist World." *Cambridge University Press, B.J. Pol. S. 33.* 2003, pp. 635–657.

Frost, Robert. "The Road Not Taken." Bartleby.com. 25 January 2009. http://www.bartleby.com/104.67.html

Gallup. "Just One in Four Urban Cubans Satisfied with Personal Freedoms." December 2006. http://www.gallup.com/poll/25915/just-one-four-urban-cubans-satisfied-personal-freedoms.aspx

Gibran, Kahlil. *The Prophet.* New York. Alfred A Knopf. 1991: 53

Gjelten, Tom. *Bacardi and the Long Fight for Cuba.* New York. Viking. 2008, p. 174

Gomez, Andy S. "The Role of Education in Cuba's Future." *ICCAS.* 2008: 7

Gomez, Andy S. and Rothe, Eugenio M. "Value Orientations and Opinions of Recently Arrived Cubans in Miami." *ICCAS.* 2004.

Gonzalez-Corzo, Mario A. and Susel Perez. *Comparative Analysis of Purchasing Power in Cuba.* Miami. Institute for Cuban and Cuban-American Studies. May 2009.

Gutiérrez-Boronat, Orlando. *La República Invisible.* Rodes Printing: 123 Hayek, F.A. Law, Legislation and Liberty, Vol. II, p. 86 as quoted by Thomas Sowell, Kindle location 1808.

Hernández-Catá, Ernesto. *Institutions to Accompany the Market in Cuba's Future Economic Tranistion.* Miami. Cuba Transition Project. 2005, p. 5.

Inglehart, Ronald and Klingemann, Hans-Dieter. "Genes, Culture, Democracy, and Happiness." in E. Diener and E. M. Suh (eds) Culture and Subjective Well-Being, pp. 165–183. Cambridge, MA: MIT Press. 2000.

Jacobs, Garry and Harland Cleveland. "Social Development Theory." *International Center for Peace and Development (ICPD)*, November 1, 1999.

James C. Davies, "Toward a Theory of Revolution." *American Sociological Review*, 27.1 (1962): 5–19.

Jorge, Antonio. *Privatization, Reconstruction, and Socio-Economic Development in Post-Castro Cuba*. Miami. Cuba Transition Project. 2003, p. 18.

Kollbrunner, Marcus. "50 Years since the Cuban Revolution." *China Worker*. 11 January 2009. London. 20 January 2009. Chinaworker.org/en/content/news/608/

Kornai, Janos. *What can Countries Embarking on Post-Socialist Transformation Learn from the Experiences so Far?* Miami. Cuba Transition Project. 2004, p. 24.

Kroll, Luisa. "The World's Billionaires 2008." *Forbes*. 5 March 2008. http://www.forbes.com/lists/2008/03/05/richest-people-billionaires-billionaires08-cx_lk_0305billie_land.html.

Latell, Brian. *The Cuban Military and Transition Dynamics*. Miami. Cuba Transition Project. 2003. http://ctp.iccas.miami.edu/Research_Studies/BLatell.pdf

Madison, James. "The Federalist No.10." *Daily Advertiser*. November 1787. http://www.constitution.org/fed/federa10.htm

Magalhanes, Pedro C. "The Politics of Judicial Reform in Eastern Europe." *Comparative Politics*. October 1999, pp. 43–62.

Manzetti, Luigi. "Political Manipulations and Market Reforms Failures." *World Politics 55*. April 2003, pp. 315–60.

Montaner, Carlos Alberto. *La Libertad y sus Enemigos*. Editorial Sudamérica. Buenos Aires 2005: p. 13

Montaner, Carlos Alberto. *The Spanish Transition and the Case of Cuba*. Miami. Institute for Cuban and Cuban- American Studies. 2002. http://ctp.iccas.miami.edu/research_studies/camontaner.pdf

Mujal-León, Eusebio. "Can Cuba Change? Tensions in the Regime." *Journal of Democracy*. 20,1. January 2009: 20–35.

Nelson, Joan M. "The Politics of Economic Transformation: Is Third World Experience Relevant in Eastern Europe?" *World Politics 45*. April 1993, pp. 433–63.

Pedraza, Silvia. "Cuba's Refugees: Manifold Migrations." *ASCE*. 1995

Perez Jr., Louis A. *To Die in Cuba, Suicide and Society*. Chapell Hill. University of North Carolina Press. 2005: 5

Ripoll, Carlos, ed. *Marti, Thoughts/Pensamientos A Bilingual Anthology*. New York. Eliseo Torres & Sons. 1985

Roig, Pedro. *Death of a Dream: History of Cuba*. Miami: Rodes Press, 2008: 174

Rummel, Rudolf, J. *Power Kills: Democracy as a Method of Nonviolence*. New Brunswick. Transaction, 1997.

Sanchez, Yoani. "Reloj de Arena." *Generación Y*. February, 2009. http://www.desdecuba.com/generaciony/?p=706

Shakespeare, William. *The Tempest*, act II, scene I, lines 253–54.

Shermer, Michael. *The Mind of the Market*. New York. Times Books, Henry Hold and Company, LLC. 2008.

Sowell, Thomas. *A Conflict of Visions: Ideological Origins of Political Struggles*. New York: Basic Books. 2007. Kindle location 39

Suchlicki, Jaime. *Cuba: From Columbus to Castro and Beyond*. Washington, D.C.: Brassey's, INC, 2000: 115

Thaler, Richard H and Cass R. Sunstein. *Nudge: Improving Decisions about Health, Wealth, and Happiness*. New Haven. Yale University Press. 2008

De Tocqueville, Alexis. *The Old Regime and the French Revolution* (trans. by John Bonner), N.Y.: Harper & Bros., 1856: 214. As quoted by James C. Davies.

Welsh, Helga A. "Political Transition Processes in Central and Eastern Europe." *Comparative Politics*. July 1994, pp. 379–394.

Weyland, Kurt. "The Political Fate of Market Reform in Latin America, Africa, and Eastern Europe." *International Studies Quarterly*. 1998, 42, pp. 645–674.

World Health Organization. "Suicide Rates in Cuba, 1963–2005." Suicide Prevention and Special Programmes. 24 January 2009. http://www.who.int/mental_health/media/cuba.pdf

About the Author

José Azel left Cuba in 1961 as a thirteen-year-old political exile in what has been dubbed Operation Pedro Pan—the largest unaccompanied child refugee movement in the history of the Western hemisphere. He is currently dedicated to the in-depth analyses of Cuba's economic, social, and political state, with a keen interest in post-Castro Cuba strategies as a Senior Scholar at the Institute for Cuban and Cuban-American Studies (ICCAS) at the University of Miami and has published extensively on Cuba related topics.

Dr. Azel was one of the founders of Pediatrix Medical Group, the nation's leading provider of pediatric specialty services, and served as its first chief financial officer. He co-founded and serves as board chairman of Children's Center for Development and Behavior, an organization dedicated to providing therapies for children with autism and other pervasive developmental disorders. Dr. Azel was an Adjunct Professor of International Business at the School of Business Administration, Department of Management, University of Miami.

He holds undergraduate and master's degrees in business administration and a PhD in International Affairs from the University of Miami. Dr. Azel has a comprehensive general management background integrating broad functional experience in corporate governance, organizational development, and finance.

Praise for Mañana in Cuba

"MUCH HAS BEEN WRITTEN ABOUT Cuba's past but, sadly, very little about its future, its challenges, or its potential - until now! In *Mañana in Cuba*, Dr. Jose Azel gives us a uniquely thoughtful and insightful view of a post-communist Cuba. A great accomplishment and a must read for anyone interested in Cuba and our Hemisphere."

—Carlos M. Gutierrez, 35th U.S. Secretary of Commerce and former Chairman of the Board and CEO of the Kellogg Company

"Dr. Azel is a brilliant thinker. In his book *Mañana in Cuba* he helps us explore in a precise, methodical manner the intelligent solutions to the many challenges that will have to be confronted by the Cuban people when the sun finally rises on a post-Castro Cuba."

—Roger J. Medel MD, Chief Executive Officer, Mednax, Inc.

"This magnificent book admirably develops the thesis that 'A successful Cuban transition must focus above all on developing a framework of democratic empowerment and a culture of tolerance,' and shows how freedom can be nurtured and citizens nudged to support it. A must read for those interested in Cuba's future."

—Ambassador James C. Cason, former Chief of Mission, USINT, Havana, Cuba

"Sophisticated, balanced, and nuanced, this elegantly written analysis deserves a large audience on all sides of the Cuba debates."

—Brian Latell, author of, *After Fidel, Raul Castro and the Future of Cuba's Revolution*, (Palgrave, 2005)

"A superb analysis of contemporary Cuba and of the issues facing a post-Castro era. A must read for those in government, business and academia interested in Cuba's future."

—Jaime Suchlicki, Emilio Bacardi Moreau Distinguished Professor, University of Miami

"Dr. Azel's book critically analyzes the challenges and opportunities Cuba faces in its future by making his readers think 'outside the box.' A must read."

—Andy S. Gomez, Associate Provost, University of Miami

"Dr. Jose Azel has given us a rare jewel with this book: a passionate, rigorous work which ably separates facts from values and dares to make an in-depth prognosis of Cuba's political body now and in the post-Castro era. Azel has made an unequivocal contribution to rationality in Cuban politics in the 21st century."

—Orlando Gutierrez-Boronat, Visiting Professor of Political Science, Florida International University

Index